Dedication

To the hundreds of individuals I have had the privilege of working with in my role as teacher, psychologist and psychotherapist. I have been privy to sharing some of their innermost struggles and difficulties, their triumphs and successes. Their bravery in coming forward to want to make some sense of their lives and gain insight, to be open to new ways of thinking is a testimony to their hard work and commitment. For the tensions, tears, anxieties, and worries we have worked through, I dedicate this book to your determination and authenticity. For the laughter we have shared as insights are gained and life is put into a new perspective.

To all the researchers, academics, writers, philosophers, health care professionals and educationalists, whose common aim is to help others to maximize their wellbeing, health and happiness.

I have listened to many moving life stories, anecdotes and personal journeys. I truly believe a person has the inner resources to be able to flourish in life. Sometimes, we can do with some help along the way. If you can take a ___ ___ strategies, technique ___ ___ hen I will have achieve ___

I have been fortunate to be able to study and learn from great teachers, colleagues, friends and family over the years. My goal has been to share some of this with you.

Thank you to all those whose work I have drawn upon, whose lives I have shared.

A man is but the product of his thoughts, what he thinks, he becomes.

Mahatma Ghandi

Gill Garratt, November 2012

Contents

Introduction

What is Cognitive Behavioural Therapy or CBT?

Men are disturbed not by things but by the views which they take of them.

Epictetus

Having picked this book up you may already have heard a little about Cognitive Behavioural Therapy. CBT has become very popular in the 21st century, with research showing that it is a very effective form of therapy for helping with many psychological struggles. It can help reduce anxiety, depression, anger, guilt, low self-esteem, phobias, obsessive behaviour, panic attacks, traumatic stress disorder and many other conditions of emotional upset. More and more integrated healthcare systems are using CBT to help people deal with everyday struggles.

CBT stands for:

Cognitive – thinking
Behavioural – behaviour
Therapy – change

CBT is about how changing your thinking can help you to tackle and overcome any negative behaviours or habits that you may have, which are getting in the way of you leading a happy life. We all have the ability to wind ourselves up with our thinking, and sometimes you may get stuck in 'thinking loops' that are unhelpful – letting the same cycle of negative thoughts go round and round in your head.

But we don't need to be slaves to this. If you realize that you are stuck in problematic thinking loops that are upsetting you or making your life more difficult, it is possible to stop and work them out. There are practical techniques you can learn in order to make conscious choices to change that thinking. This book will help you recognize when life is getting tough for you and provide you with practical strategies to stop things escalating and getting out of control.

The title of this book is *CBT for Work*, and so it will concentrate in particular on showing how CBT can help you reduce the time you spend worrying about work and work-related circumstances. Many of us work in hectic, high-pressure environments, and find that the changing demands of our job are a frequent source of hassle and stress. Of course it is natural to have a healthy concern about your work performance, job prospects and career, but it is not in your best interests to worry yourself so much that you make yourself ill. It is important to find a balance between having a healthy commitment to your work and suffering from overriding anxiety as a result of being over-invested in it.

CBT also looks at resilience. We can all expect to go through some difficult patches in life – it's unavoidable.

Although CBT can help you to change negative thinking into more positive thinking, it does stress that sometimes we need to go through discomfort zones in order to progress in life. CBT can help increase your ability to tolerate the tough times without freezing with fear or crumpling under the pressures. As Winston Churchill famously said: 'When you are going through hell, keep going.'

CBT can be used with emotional struggles of differing intensities, but in all cases the same basic techniques apply. Depending on the level of distress, CBT in conjunction with medicine may be recommended by doctors. This combination has been found to be highly effective for treating anxiety and depression. This book is certainly not intended to take the place of proper medical attention, and if you become truly worried about your ability to cope with a situation you should visit your doctor immediately. However, if you have some knowledge and understanding of CBT you will find that in many situations you are able to help yourself. CBT has been widely researched and tested, many scientific papers have been published and it is the preferred choice of many health organizations worldwide. It is an effective tool for dealing with the pressures of a modern working environment and if you learn to use it you will not only be happier but also, as a result of not being dogged by constant worries, a more effective employee.

This book will include:

- Where CBT came from

- How to recognize if you are getting stressed

- Your CBT 'Think Kit', a practical toolkit to teach you the basic ABC of CBT

- You and your Work

- Common problems in the workplace – anxiety, anger, guilt, depression, low self-esteem

- How to use your CBT 'Think Kit' for work

- Maximizing your happiness at work

- Balancing work and life

- Taking CBT further

Where did CBT come from?

There are many other types of therapy besides CBT that have evolved over the 20th century. As the study of psychology has become more popular many different methods for treating emotional difficulties have been put forward. This can sometimes be rather confusing. Before we start looking at the practical applications of CBT it is probably a good idea to explain how it was developed, in order to place it in context. What follows is a (necessarily very brief) history of therapy.

Freud (1856–1939) was a medical doctor, and one of the first scientists to become interested in studying human behaviour. He realized that some of his patients were showing signs of illness without an obvious physical cause and began to direct his attention to the study of the mind. He started to study human emotional development and concluded that some people may not develop in healthy ways, and that this could affect them for the rest of their lives. When people struggled, and perhaps exhibited 'hysterical', 'repressed' or 'displacement' behaviours, he thought it was a symptom of deeper unresolved problems. Freud recommended analysis of their childhood development to find where the blockages had occurred. This technique was called 'psychoanalysis'. His theories and treatments had a huge impact on society at the time and have continued to greatly influence psychology as well as permeating many aspects of culture including art and literature.

Behaviour therapy developed when other psychologists in history wanted to learn more about the mechanisms of behaviour. A Russian psychologist called Pavlov (1849–1936) discovered that if he rang a bell when he gave food to a dog on enough occasions, eventually the dog would salivate in anticipation of getting food when it heard the bell, even if no food accompanied it. He called this a 'conditioned reflex'. This knowledge has since been used in all sorts of situations to reinforce behaviours in humans too. If humans are rewarded with praise or 'treats' they are likely to repeat the behaviour they have been rewarded for. If we are rewarded with a bonus for being more productive at work, we are likely to want to repeat that behaviour. This is called positive reinforcement. On the flipside, it is theoretically also possible to use punishment in order to eliminate behaviour which is seen as unacceptable, though if we are applying that to the world of work it seems a rather scary management style!

In short, then, the aim of this kind of therapy is to change the behaviour of the subject (the clue is in the name!). It was then used for the treatment of people who suffered from 'disorders' of the mind, to train them to behave in more acceptable ways. An interesting point to note about treating people in this way is that although the treatment may often have changed their behaviour, it did not necessarily seem to get to the origin of their difficulties. That is to say, subjects treated with behaviour therapy do get into new habits of behaviour, but without really thinking about it.

Cognitive therapy was the next stage in considering human behaviour. In the 1940s there was a lot of interest in trying to understand the motivation *behind* people's behaviours – something that was arguably lacking from behaviour therapy. It was noticed that although you could train people to behave differently, some continued to experience 'disorders' or to revert to previous problematic patterns of behaviour after a time.

Depression and anxiety were two areas of particular interest. A pioneer in this area was a psychoanalyst called

Dr Aaron Beck, who noticed that his depressed patients seemed to think in similar ways. This included thinking negatively about themselves, the world in general and about their futures – they seemed to have got into the habit of thinking negatively. In the 1960s he started therapy programmes to help patients to identify their negative thoughts, to recognize that their thinking patterns had become 'distorted' from reality and to help them challenge these errors in their thinking.

While some attention was paid to the individual's past, in order to see how they could have got into these negative thinking patterns, the main emphasis was on working in the present. The person's thinking, or 'beliefs', about themselves, the world or their hopeless future could be challenged by working with their therapist. This could be the start of them breaking their cycles of repetitive, automatic, negative thinking and replacing them with more positive thinking. The more we think we are useless and avoid activities which we fear could confirm this negative view of ourselves, the more we seem to prove the validity of that view – we ensure that we 'fail' by never letting ourselves try. This causes us to perpetuate depression or escalate anxiety. We can get carried away with our negative thinking and 'catastrophize' what will happen in the future. By interacting with a cognitive therapist, the habit of negative thinking could be broken and feelings of anxiety and depression could be reduced.

Cognitive Behavioural Therapy was developed from the Rational Emotive Behaviour Therapy, first proposed in 1955 by Dr Albert Ellis (1913–2007). This combination therapy integrated the findings from behaviour therapy and cognitive therapy, working on the basis that our thinking, our physical states and our behaviours all interact. Mind and body influence each other, and our behaviour is the result of our thinking and our constantly changing body chemistry. The way we think affects what goes on in our bodies. For example, if you suddenly have anxious thoughts, your body reacts by releasing higher quantities of particular hormones into your blood stream, which in turn affect the way you feel and so your behaviour. Here is a brief summary of how CBT works:

- Your thinking is the result of how you view yourself, the world and your future. You may think negatively at times, and may interpret threats in your world.

- When you think you are threatened, your body will react. These changes in your body will in turn affect the way you feel, and so your behaviour. All of this will seem to reinforce the validity of the negative thinking that started the process, trapping you in an unhelpful thinking loop which will lead to further negative feelings and behaviour … and so it goes on.

- You probably can't change whatever it is that is going on in your world which you perceive as a threat, at least not straight away. But you can change the way you think about yourself, the world and the future.

- If you change the way you think, you will change the way you feel, and change the way you behave. You can break the unhelpful thinking loop.

- CBT can help you work out what you are feeling.

- CBT can help you work out what is triggering upsetting feelings.

- CBT can help you work out your thinking.

- CBT gives you choices and practical strategies to change your thinking and so reduce upset.

This book is a practical guide to CBT techniques that can be used to help you work your way through difficulties in your life, particularly with regard to work. We will look first at identifying when you are in difficulty and what in particular is problematic, after which you can begin to use the **CBT Think Kit** to help reduce your unhelpful thinking. The CBT Think Kit is explained in the next chapter. It gives you a simple, logical way to help you work through tough times and uncomfortable feelings. It puts you in control – you make the choices to decide to help yourself to a calmer state.

This book will use plenty of examples to show you how the Think Kit can be used. These examples will be related to problems commonly experienced at work. You will also be given opportunities to use your own experiences and apply the CBT Think Kit to them. The more you practise CBT, the easier it becomes.

 CBT is for Life, not just for crises.

Important note
This book will look at the everyday problems and upsets in our working lives. It is important that you always consult your doctor if your negative feelings persist for a significant length of time. We will concentrate on the most commonly occurring negative feelings – things which are moderately upsetting, everyday stresses. If you start to feel overwhelmed, or recognize that you are experiencing extremes of the symptoms listed in the next chapter, it is essential to contact a health professional. It can be helpful to write down what has been happening, and perhaps to take a friend along too – when we are feeling distressed it can sometimes be hard to explain things to a doctor without becoming upset. This book will help you see that it is natural to become upset sometimes in our lives, and that this is nothing to be ashamed of. It will show you how to recognize the symptoms and do something about them before they spiral out of control.

The key points

- CBT is just one form of psychological therapy

- Different therapies stem from different psychological theories

- Psychoanalysis, Behavioural Therapy and Cognitive Therapy are just three of many

- CBT is becoming increasingly popular

- CBT is a practical therapy

- You can learn some CBT basics and help yourself to reduce upsetting feelings and enhance positive feelings

- You can carry your own CBT Toolkit with you to make adjustments to your emotional wellbeing

- You can use your toolkit at work and for your personal life

1. The CBT Think Kit

Big jobs usually go to the men who prove their ability to outgrow the small ones.

Ralph Waldo Emerson

The more you understand about yourself and how you think, the more power you will have to change the way you live. And by using the systems of CBT you are giving yourself the advantage of years of research done by other people; specialists who have devoted their lives to understanding more about how we work. You don't need to be a trained mechanic in order to be able to drive a car – though some basic knowledge of how an engine works is very helpful – but you do still need to be taught. In exactly the same way, you don't need to know all about every piece of research into CBT that has been done in order to be able to utilize it in your own life. But you do still need to be taught.

Now that the introduction has equipped you with a basic knowledge of the theory behind CBT it's time to get in the metaphorical driving seat and have a look at how it can work in practice. We will now look at a simple technique which will help you to work out the links between particular thoughts and your feeling upset, and which will show you how to tackle the problem. I call it the CBT Think Kit and have used it with many clients to solve issues in both their personal and professional lives.

It is a practical toolkit that can help you work out your difficulties and take action to reduce them. It includes an A, B, C, framework to work with, which will hopefully make things easier to remember:

A is the actual **situation** that gives rise to the thinking.

B is the **belief** you may hold about the situation you experience

C is the **consequence** of you hanging on to those beliefs. The consequences can be feelings and behaviours.

THINK ABOUT IT

Suppose you have been sent on an important business trip and because of a problem with your train, you arrive at the airport late. Then, to make matters worse, there is a **situation** (A) at the check-in desk – someone jumps the queue in front of you. As a **consequence** (C) you may feel angry about that. But CBT encourages you to realize that it is not actually the person jumping the queue (A) that is making you angry. There is a B that comes between A and C. In fact, it is your **beliefs** (B) about how the world should be fair which are at the root of your anger. The person behind you may not be at all bothered about the person jumping the queue. He or she may view the situation differently and so also feel differently – they may be quite calm, perhaps irritated but certainly not angry. Your *thoughts* will trigger your feelings of anger and resentment. It is not actually the person jumping the queue that is causing your anger. It is more your view about how people *should* behave ...

In this situation the big question is: how is it helping *you* to keep thinking like that?

You don't have to upset yourself. Although you feel very strongly about fairness and justice, sometimes it may not be in your own best interests in a particular situation if you allow such beliefs and get into a state of anxiety or unhappiness. True, perhaps it would be appropriate to step in and ask the person to take their proper place in the queue, but if you do not want or are unable to do this then getting worked up is unproductive.

People seem to be very good at beating themselves up. You are often your own harshest critic.

People are upset not by the things that happen to them, or by the actions and behaviours of other people, but by the opinion that they come to have about it all. No one else upsets you; you do it to yourself.

The importance of your thinking

Your thinking is reflected in how you behave. If you are worried about something, you tend to think about it a lot. You can make yourself anxious or upset and this may show in your behaviour. You may become clumsy, feel hot and sweaty, appear tearful, get annoyed with others, or sulk. As a result you may make mistakes or rash decisions, or else alienate people. You may find yourself suffering from disturbed sleep patterns, changing your eating and drinking habits, and generally not feeling yourself.

It's not difficult to see that as well as being unpleasant for you to have to experience this kind of thing in itself, it is also likely to be detrimental to your work. By tackling negative thoughts and beliefs head on you are also giving yourself the best conditions to perform well in your job. In cases where your beliefs and anxieties relate to not being good enough at your job, that's killing two birds with one stone!

A consciousness of wrongdoing is the first step to salvation ... you have to catch yourself doing it before you can correct it.

Seneca

Think of something that 'made' you feel anxious recently at work. It could be having a disagreement with a colleague, being late for a meeting, losing an important document, going for a job interview, or over-spending on a project. Think about it for a few seconds and try to picture the situation in as much detail as possible. How did it feel? You may even experience some of those flutters of anxiety again just from recalling it.

On a scale of 1–5, how anxious did you feel then?

1 stands for slightly concerned, 2 irritated, 3 annoyed, 4 agitated and 5 anxious.

All of those feelings include an element of feeling uncomfortable. Each person's tolerance level varies. It could be that you generally have a low tolerance and find yourself getting anxious, or angry, or upset quite quickly. CBT can help you to raise your tolerance levels by training you to stop yourself from escalating into that discomfort zone.

Let's look at the Think Kit again. This model can be used at any time you are feeling upset, from mild to strong feelings. It is up to you to decide if you are feeling upset and if you want to reduce the imbalance and discomfort.

Remember the ABC framework

A is the letter representing the **actual event or the trigger that led to you feeling upset**.

B is the **belief or view** we hold about the event.

C is the **consequence** of the event, this could be **an emotional consequence, a behavioural consequence, or both**.

A does **NOT** cause **C**

It is not an event or another person (A) that makes you feel upset (C).

There is always something between the A and the C which we need to take into account. The B stands for – our belief, view or opinion relating to the A, the actual event. It is this that gives rise to the emotional or behavioural consequences you experience, the C. These beliefs are our opinions and values; ways we think about the world or about other people. Some examples might be:

'I believe people should stick to their decisions'
'I think that I should always be on time'
'I believe that we must show respect for each other'

An easy way to spot your own beliefs is to look out for words such as 'should', 'ought' or 'must'.

The power of these beliefs

You may have firm views about how others should behave, how the world should treat you and about fairness and justice.

For example, you may believe that people should keep to an arrangement once it's been made. When a colleague emails to say they are no longer able to help you on a particular project, you may get a flash of emotion. You are angry that she has let you down, 'How dare she break an arrangement and leave me in the lurch! I wouldn't do that. She obviously doesn't care at all about how that affects me – it's really mean and unfair.' As long as you hang on to your view of how she *should have* behaved, you continue to upset yourself.

Many of your views about how to behave start in childhood. Sometimes, as adults, we may discover that hanging on to very rigid beliefs may not be helpful. If you find that you are often upsetting yourself you may want to consider adjusting your views. This is not to say that you should be encouraged not to care about anything and become totally self-centred. Nor should anyone feel that they have to compromise conscientious beliefs which are important to them. Rather, we should all work towards having an 'enlightened self interest'. This means being aware of your views in a given situation, in order to be able to control the effect they have on you for the sake of maximizing happiness and minimizing upset in any given circumstance.

Here is another example I use with clients to demonstrate 'unhelpful beliefs'.

A tale of two journeys

Jeff, who had a new car, was driving to work when a car pulled out in front of him and just missed hitting him. Jeff shouted, 'Silly idiot, you nearly took my front wing off! You shouldn't be allowed on the road!' He waved his fist at this other car and became red in the face. He was sweating and his eyes were bulging. He carried on to work, parked, slammed his door shut and strode into the office, still furious. He went to his desk, dumped his bag on it, fired up his computer and marched off to make a cup of coffee. He met a colleague in the kitchen and loudly told him about the incident, not even bothering to say hello first. Every time he thought about what had happened that morning, he became angry.

Simon, who worked with Jeff, also had a new car. When he was driving to work in the morning, a car also pulled out right in front of him, just missing him. Simon said quietly to himself, 'Phew, close one. That could have been nasty. There are some careless drivers on the road.' He carried on to work, parked, closed the door quietly and went into work. He got some water from the cooler, greeted his colleagues and sat down at his desk.

How would you describe Jeff's feelings about the incident? What do you think the main emotion he felt was? How would you describe Simon's feelings about the incident ? How did his response differ from Jeff's?

There was certainly a difference in how the two men reacted, and so we can infer that there must also have been a difference in their thoughts about the event. Jeff seemed to react much more strongly, with anger. He clearly had a

strong belief that people should not drive in that danger-
ous way. That's not particularly unusual – I'm sure we can all
agree with that sentiment. However, he then held on to that
belief, despite the fact that the event had passed and there
was nothing he could do to change it. As long as he held
on to that strong belief and kept thinking back on what had
happened, he kept himself wound up about it.

Simon did not seem to hold such strong beliefs. He certainly had a sensible preference that other drivers should
drive carefully, but the incident had happened. There was
no point going around insisting that other drivers should
always drive carefully. The evidence showed that this guy
hadn't, and that was that. Simon had a preference, but if
the evidence showed that others didn't drive the way he
preferred, well it was inconvenient and alarming at the time
but the deed was done.

They both had a choice.

Jeff was perhaps justifiably angry about the behaviour
of the other driver initially, but he refused to let go of his
strong beliefs about the way people should drive. Simon
accepted that things didn't always happen the way he
would like. He was slightly annoyed, but how would making himself angry about it help him? It wouldn't.

How could Jeff stop himself feeling angry? He could
change the way he viewed the situation. It takes hard work
to change the way we view things. It involves changing our
beliefs about how other people should be, how the world
should be and also how we should be in the world. But

it can be done, and CBT gives us the toolkit to apply to the problem.

 It is not people or events that upset us, we do that all by ourselves.

Now let's put Jeff and Simon into the ABC framework of the Think Kit.

The actual event (A) was the car pulling out. The consequences (C), were their feelings and behaviours: anger and accompanying physical symptoms for Jeff, annoyance for Simon.

But it wasn't the car pulling out (A) that caused the feelings. If it was, Jeff and Simon would have felt exactly the same. There is something in between A and C – their differing beliefs (B).

Jeff believed A *should* not happen – a strong belief

Simon *preferred* that A should not happen, but did not hold onto a strong belief about it.

What happens at B determines the outcome at C.

The Universe is change, life is an opinion

Marcus Aurelius

22

How we think determines how we feel

Emotional consequences in difficult situations can be considered in terms of upsetting emotions and less upsetting emotions. Jeff's anger was an upsetting emotion. Simon's annoyance was a less upsetting emotion – he didn't like what happened, but it didn't affect him deeply.

If we consider these emotions on a sliding scale, since they represent degrees of intensity of similar feelings, we can see that while Simon felt irritated and annoyed, he didn't slide further up the scale to anger in the way that Jeff did.

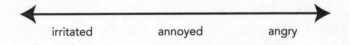

irritated   annoyed   angry

Learning to identify your own feelings

It's not difficult to see how being free from being controlled by rigid beliefs could be a good thing. It could allow you to keep your cool when under a tight deadline, or to remain calm and in control when dealing with a difficult colleague. But how do you even start to change your beliefs in this way? It takes a lot of practice to make the cognitive shift from a strong belief to a preference. Before you get to this stage, however, you need to be able to identify times when you are feeling unusually upset, and identify the beliefs that contribute to them. Let's consider a situation from your past.

Think of a time when you felt upset. Now go through the following process:

Step 1
- Identify the A, the actual situation that triggered these feelings.

Step 2
- Identify the C, the consequences – exactly how you felt and behaved.

Step 3
- Now what was the B, the belief or beliefs, that caused you to feel that way? If you are finding it difficult to work out, look out for 'should', 'ought' or 'must' in your thinking. Say it out loud, if that helps: 'I/he/she/they should not …'

It can be quite hard to put a name to your feelings. To help you I have put together a list of words that may help to describe some common feelings and which often point to particular emotional states. They may be useful when you are trying to identify specifically how you are feeling when you are in some way out of balance about something.

Anxiety:
Uneasy, unsettled, restless, agitated, bothered, tense, worried, anxious

Fear:
Nervous, alarmed, insecure, fearful, threatened, vulnerable, frightened, panicky

Anger:
Disappointed, frustrated, annoyed, upset, indignant, defiant, hostile, aggravated, disgusted, furious, vengeful, outraged, fuming

Guilt
Troubled, humble, flustered, embarrassed, regretful, remorseful, worthless

Depression
Sad, low, melancholy, unhappy, miserable, weepy, dismal, lethargic, bored, exhausted, detached, hopeless, despairing, suicidal

Low self-esteem
Weak, helpless, powerless, lonely, passive, lost, pessimistic, selfish, ungrounded, humiliated, inadequate, pointless

The way I have categorized that list is not incidental. I have found from working with clients that there are five main areas where people struggle. This list is not a comprehensive one of all the issues that CBT can help with, but it is a good starting point for you to get to grips with. So the particular forms of difficulty we will be focusing on are:

- anxiety and fear
- anger and frustration
- guilt
- depression
- low self-esteem

These seem to be common upsetting feelings which can interfere with your personal, professional and social life.

To help to picture how CBT works, I sometimes use the analogy of keeping a car running smoothly. Just as a car may start showing warning signs of struggling by making funny noises, burning oil, squeaky brakes or stalling so your body may show you signs of wear and tear that are an indication that you have been having a difficult time emotionally. When you are feeling out of kilter, you may find you experience some of these physical and mental symptoms, and these can be another good way of identifying that you have a problem if you are in the habit of second guessing yourself and do not feel able to make an accurate assessment of your feelings. Obviously a lot of these symptoms can also be related to other medical conditions and therefore you should always consult a medical professional if symptoms persist.

Physical symptoms

- headaches
- breathlessness, a lump in the throat
- dizziness
- palpitations
- diarrhoea, flatulence, constipation
- backaches
- wanting to urinate more often
- blood pressure changes
- sleep problems
- visual disturbances
- butterflies in the stomach, nausea, indigestion
- tiredness, exhaustion
- changes in eating patterns, loss of appetite
- frequent small illnesses such as colds
- increased alcohol consumption, loss of libido
- cold hands and feet
- tenseness in muscles, aches and pains
- sweatiness, feeling flushed
- jaw tenseness and grinding of teeth
- nail biting, finger and feet tapping, trembling hands

Behavioural symptoms

- Finding it difficult to concentrate, forgetfulness, lack of motivation, procrastination, loss of creativity
- Getting easily irritated, impatient, hostile or angry
- Rushing into things, trying to do too much at once
- Being more accident prone than usual
- Not finishing tasks, flitting about from one job to another
- Spending excessive time on social media sites
- Overreacting to feedback
- Getting bored easily
- Making rigid demands of yourself and others; being critical and unbending
- Being inefficient in everyday life
- Allowing things to pile up and not knowing where to start

 Can you recognize yourself suffering from any of these symptoms? If so then you may be suffering from some form of distress which you have ignored up to this point.

 Keep a feelings diary of when you experience any of the symptoms. Look back over a week and see when these feelings occur and how

28

often they crop up. It is worth doing this to help you identify **what the situation** is that triggers your anxiety
response. This can be the first step in realizing you have a
problem.

If you've had a fairly calm and relaxed week the chances are
you will not have experienced many of these symptoms, if
any. When we have a holiday we often find we are pleas-
antly surprised at how many of our problems seem to fade.
But if you've had a busy week full of demands and jobs to
be done, it could be that you experience quite a few of
these uncomfortable symptoms

Nicky used to love her job and looked forward to
the new week; getting her work organized and
having a chance to catch up with her colleagues
in the lunch break. However, there had been
some restructuring a few months previously
which meant that she had a new manager. This manager
had reorganized the department and changed the sched-
ules. Nicky's role now included collating the sales figures
from the previous week and presenting them to the whole
team on a Monday morning. There was now a rota for coffee and lunch breaks to ensure that there were always staff
available to receive calls. Nicky was not on the same breaks
as her friends. Nicky started to dread going back to work

after the weekend and would start feeling sick and tearful on a Sunday night.

Nicky was suffering from physical and behavioural symptoms. Such signs of imbalance are often associated with continuing anxiety, anger, fear, frustration and guilt. You may not always be aware that you are worrying but it will take its toll nonetheless. Studies show that feeling guilty for a long time can affect the chemicals in your body. Serotonin is the 'happy hormone', responsible for a sense of well-being. When your serotonin levels are low you may feel less happy than usual, or even depressed.

There are sound evolutionary reasons for there to be a link between your thinking and your body's internal chemistry. You may, for example, have heard of the 'fight or flight' response. It is a reaction whereby when we feel threatened we receive a boost of adrenaline in order to prime our muscles to fight off any aggressors or else to flee from danger. There are rarely grizzly bears to contend with these days but the mechanism remains. While the 'threat' of having to give a work presentation in front of a large group of people is not a matter of life or death, such scenarios can still cause the same response.

It can be helpful to have a basic understanding of the body's reactions, as it may help us to rationalize sudden, strong emotions that we may feel. Your emotions are often revealed in your blood chemistry, as the body pours different hormones into your bloodstream when you are under stress, according to how you react to it.

The stress response is largely brought about by the action of the hormones cortisol, adrenaline and noradrenaline:

When you get **angry** there is a large increase in *noradrenaline* – this primes you to fight.

When you are **fearful** there is a large increase in *adrenaline* – this primes you to run away.

When you are **depressed** there is a large increase in *cortisol* – this primes you to be submissive.

And on the more positive side of things:

When you are **calm** there is a decrease in noradrenaline – this allows relaxation and serenity.

When you are **happy** there are changes in the level of testosterone which can induce feelings of love and security. Testosterone is a well-known hormone responsible for the development of male sexual characteristics. It has been seen that it affects the emotional states of men and women in different ways when involved in attraction. Men are found to have decreasing levels of testosterone when they fall in love and women to have increasing levels. Fatherhood also reduces levels in men. Being involved in competitive activities can raise levels of testosterone and as this happens a person can exhibit more risk-taking behaviour and be more aggressive. This is interesting to bear in mind when working in a competitive environment – healthy competition may give some people an edge, but if the levels get out of balance, the attendant risk-taking behaviour could have detrimental results. A study by Paul Zak in 2009 also showed that when testosterone levels increase in men they are more likely to behave in a selfish way and to punish others for acting in what they perceive to be a selfish way towards them.

Let's look at each in a little more detail.

Noradrenaline

This is the hormone associated with aggression and fighting. The physical effects are tenseness in facial muscles, clenching of teeth, hairs standing on end, skin becoming sweaty, blood vessels constricting, the pupils of the eyes dilating. The person feels more alert; ready to do battle. When there is no situation that causes anger, noradrenaline can make you feel excited and happy.

Adrenaline

This is the hormone that prepares the body to run away. Blood is diverted to large muscles to prepare them for use, and as it drains away again, you may experience butterflies, a cold sweat can break out, and you may have the feeling of a knot in the stomach. This is the hormone that is being secreted when you have feelings of worry and anxiety.

Cortisol

It is harder to outwardly spot when cortisol is being secreted into the bloodstream. Long term secretion of cortisol can lower your immunoglobulin levels, which keep your immune system healthy. Studies indicate that frequent colds, or the worsening of asthma or allergies could be to do with cortisol levels. Feeling depressed, hopeless and having low self-esteem can also be associated with increased cortisol levels.

> *Nothing has such power to broaden the mind as the ability to investigate systematically and truly all that comes under thy observation in life.*
>
> Marcus Aurelius

Thinking outside the body

This chapter has looked at how our thinking is influenced by what is going on around us and how our body responds. How we behave is the result of a combination of influences, such as how other people treat us, what we experience in our immediate environment, our own views about the world and the chemical changes in our bodies that arise as a result of these things.

We are not aware of all of this going on; we just have to plough on, making the best decisions we can at the time. It is all too easy for things to get out of balance without us noticing; we can suddenly find ourselves struggling with difficulties which have actually been simmering under the surface for some time. These difficulties can be emotional, behavioural or physical, and are often a combination of all three.

Having read this chapter you are hopefully better equipped to work out what you are really feeling about your life and to identify the behavioural and physical warning signs of stress.

You can become your own detective, picking up clues about your emotional wellbeing. If you choose to ignore the warning signs for too long the results may become more distressing. It may feel very uncomfortable to acknowledge that something is wrong – in fact for many people it can be the hardest part of the whole process. Once you start the detective work and pay attention to what you are struggling with, you will find that you are better placed to start to calm yourself down.

In the next chapter we will look specifically at some of the challenges the workplace presents. Work can be a great source of satisfaction, pride and enjoyment, quite aside from the important fact of being paid. However, the path of our working lives is rarely that simple. There may be many challenges to face and overcome. You may face redundancy and periods of unemployment, or need to make career changes. The constant in all these situations is YOU. You can take your CBT Think Kit with you on the emotional rollercoaster of work and life, to help minimize the upset you experience during difficult times.

The key points

- Change your thinking to change the way you feel

- Identify your negative thoughts and beliefs and understand how they affect your behaviour

- Challenge your negative beliefs to change your behaviour

- Turn 'fight or flight' into 'think and stay'

- Become your own detective and learn to recognize patterns of negative thought

- Remember that you are responsible for your own emotional well-being

2. You and your work

One of the greatest of all principles is that men can do what they think they can do.

Norman Vincent Peale

The workplace today

The whole way we work has changed drastically over the last twenty years or so. It used to be the norm to have a job with set hours, in a set location – usually near to your home. People often stayed in the area where they were brought up and went to school. How things have changed today! The advances made in technology, such as 24/7 communications access mean people can work anywhere. The boundaries between work and home have become blurred. The ethos of carrying on with work in the evenings and at weekends is becoming the norm for many people. You even see people constantly checking work emails on holiday, sitting on beaches using iphones and laptops. Added to this, business now operates on a global basis and if cost effective it is not unusual for a company to decide to outsource some of their work to another country. This can create feelings of insecurity and instability for the workforce. The recent rise in unemployment in many countries has left many people feeling that they need to work even harder simply in order to keep their job.

THINK ABOUT IT

How do you feel about your job?

- Are you comfortable at work?
- Do you feel you are in the right job?
- Do you enjoy taking work home?

• Are your career prospects clear?

If you have answered 'yes' to most of the above questions then you are probably quite comfortable with your work. If you have answered 'no' to one or more then don't worry – you are not alone. Many people are struggling to keep up with the demands of the workplace.

TRY IT NOW!

Make a list of all the advantages of being in your job, and then all the disadvantages.

Advantages	Disadvantages

Look at the disadvantages column. What are the particular aspects of each item that you don't like? How do you feel when you think about them?

Perhaps you feel anxious that you are under constant pressure to meet deadlines. Maybe you feel angry that you have to spend a lot of time travelling each day to get to work. Or you may feel guilty that you quite often don't manage to complete all your tasks in the time allotted. The pressures you are under may mean that you stay awake at night worrying about how you are going to fit everything in. Perhaps you feel you are not good enough for the job, or feel your work doesn't always meet the standards you would like it to.

 CBT tells us that it is our beliefs about ourselves and our job that give rise to these uncomfortable feelings. It is how we *view* the situation at work that gives rise to our discomfort. There is nothing wrong with you. It is natural and common to worry about your job to a certain extent. However, it's very easy to work yourself up and to start worrying disproportionately. CBT can help you to put things in perspective so you don't over-worry or catastrophize to the point where you are making yourself ill.

Let's consider the challenges of the average workplace. These can include:

- Conflicts with a colleague, manager or boss

- Unrealistic workloads

- Changes in job description

- Unfairness at work – career progression, changes of role, feeling marginalized, pay issues

- Appraisals and issues of constructive feedback

- Disciplinary issues

- Changes in the company, threats of redundancy

- Managing your staff

- Meetings, presentations

- Bullying

- Dealing with mistakes

Each of those demands can be interpreted as a threat in your environment which then becomes a threat you carry in your head. The very thought of the amount of work we have to do or an upcoming appraisal meeting can be enough to set off that fight or flight reaction. The build-up of pressure sets off the anxiety symptoms.

How many of us have sat at our computers and felt frozen? Your mind goes blank, and you just keep staring at the screen. At other times when we feel threatened we involve ourselves with 'displacement' activities, like re-organizing the desk, going to the water cooler, nipping out to get a coffee or surfing the internet to distract ourselves with trivia. We look around the office and see other people apparently getting on happily with their work and we start to have doubts about ourselves.

Are you cut out for the job you are in?

Marion

Marion had worked for the same bank for twelve years when it was taken over. Many branches were shut down, including the one where Marion worked. She was offered another position in the city. It would involve two hours extra commuting time each day but since she could not afford to be without a job, she accepted. When she started work she found her role was considerably different to her previous one. She struggled to keep up with the workload her new manager had given her. She worried constantly about this and frequently felt nauseous. She was also exhausted from having to wake up early every morning. She started making more mistakes at work.

Marion began to question whether she was in the right job. She had been fine before; her work record had been excellent, she had coped well and enjoyed herself. Everything had changed so much for her and as a result of these problems she lost her confidence and felt very down.

41

In the above example it's clear that Marion was absolutely fine until she was forced to cope with a lot of change in a short space of time. The key thing to remember in CBT is that no matter how your situation may change, you are still the same person with all your skills, talents and personality traits. Sometimes we may struggle with change and begin to doubt ourselves. Marion was the same person before the job change. It was the situation that changed not her. There was nothing wrong with Marion, but the changes didn't fit with her.

The different choices we make shape the career we end up in. This is a combination of the opportunities you have in conjunction with what you decide you would like to do. With any choices you make in life, not just for work but in choosing friends, partners, social activities and everything else, your basic personality plays a large part.

Studies show that your basic personality is largely pre-defined. There have been many tests developed to identify an individual's personality. If you can have some idea of what your own is like, it can help you to accept yourself and try to find jobs that match it. If you find yourself in a job that is out of kilter with your personality that might be the reason you are unhappy. Marion was a quiet, fairly shy person who liked routine, predictability and a working day that enabled her to spend time at home. She was leaning towards the introvert end of the personality spectrum. The sudden upheavals in her working situation left her in a state of turmoil and imbalance. This job was not the one she had chosen twelve years previously; in that role she had been successful, happy and secure. She had made a suitable choice all those years ago.

All this is not to say that if you start experiencing problems at work, particularly as a result of a change of circumstances, you should immediately assume that you are a bad fit with the job and should not be working in it. It's natural to find change a little unsettling and it is very likely that in most cases after a period of adjustment we will find that we cope with a new situation fine – perhaps after applying some of the CBT techniques that we will come on to later in the book. However, it is always worth considering whether your personality really is in line with what you do. If you are a shy and introverted person you are unlikely to ever be at ease working in a job that involves making a lot of pitches or presentations, while if you are an extroverted person who enjoys a lot of contact with other people, a role involving a lot of solitary research would be unlikely to satisfy you.

This is an important theme in this book. If you can understand yourself it will help you to make suitable choices in life; ones that match up with who you are as a person.

 When choosing a job and career, if you can find one that you are really interested in and enjoy, you are more likely to be successful.

Choose a job you love and you will never have to work a day in your life.

Confucius

CASE STUDY

Tom

Tom was an IT business analyst. He was very adept at his job and in great demand. However, most of his time was spent working on his own. He started to feel ill at ease in this role and quite isolated. During one project at a hospital he was asked if he could go around the departments and talk to the doctors, nurses and administrative staff about what they wanted their new computer system to be able to do.

He made the assessment and set about implementing it ready for the launch. The head of human resources then asked if Tom might consider training the staff in the new software. Tom had really enjoyed having contact with a wide range of people during the assessment stage – they had been friendly and he had realized he had a good way of talking with people at different levels of responsibility. The training went well and Tom really enjoyed himself. As a result he gained insight into his preferred way of working – he discovered that not only was he adept at technical assessment and implementation but he also enjoyed interacting with and teaching other people. He was quite extrovert, enjoying the company of others, as well as displaying characteristics of resilience and conscientiousness in his ability to work on his own. Tom resolved that in future he would try to shift his career so that there was a greater emphasis on contact with other people, as this seemed to fit better with his personality than always working alone.

How well do you know yourself?

Answer the following questions as honestly as you can:

1. Do you like talking to lots of people?

2. Are you more likely to lead a conversation than to step back from a group and listen?

3. Do you make friends quickly and have a wide social network?

4. Do you find it difficult to stay in the background and 'go with the flow'?

5. Are you confident in groups and enjoy giving presentations?

6. Are you adept at sorting out social situations?

7. Do you find people often listen to you and look to you as a leader?

8. At work, do you get bored if you have to work quietly on your own for a long time?

If you answered mainly 'yes' to the questions above then you are likely more of an extrovert, whereas if you answered mainly 'no' then you are probably more of an introvert. Most people – about 68 per cent – fall in the middle range of the spectrum between extreme introversion and extreme extroversion.

What are extroverts like?
The characteristics of an extrovert may include:

- Becoming easily bored if no people are around

- Tending to lose energy when alone

- Being likely to think as they speak

- Actually thinking better while talking

- Enjoying social situations, and seeking the company of others

- Getting distracted easily

- Preferring to be 'on the go'.

What are introverts like?
The characteristics of an introvert may include:

- Preferring to be alone and feel energized by solitary time

- Feeling drained of energy when in hectic social situations

- Preferring considered reflection and exploration of their thoughts and feelings

- Having no problem with being alone – this does not make an introvert feel 'lonely'

- Introverts may have good social skills but prefer not to engage in trivial conversations

- Introverts choose solitary activities not because of social discomfort but as a social preference.

Other characteristics

Obviously whether someone is introverted or extroverted is only a small part of their overall personality – there are plenty of other things to take into account. Some researchers have classified personality as being made up of the 'Big Five' personality traits. Extroversion/introversion is one of them; here are the other four:

- Openness – curious and creative or more cautious and deductive

- Conscientiousness – organized and efficient or careless and easy going

- Neuroticism – confident and secure or nervous and sensitive

- Agreeableness – friendly and outgoing or cold and not empathic

As with extroversion/introversion these characteristics can all be represented on a sliding scale, with most people likely to be somewhere in the middle region between extremes. These traits can change throughout your life depending on your experiences and the particular situation you are in. The statistics given for how much these traits are pre-determined genetically range from 40–60 per cent. This is not to say that if you are born with a tendency to be more introverted and solitary that's the only way you can be; the environment you are in will influence your behaviour. We can all learn how to behave in different ways in different situations, but you will probably always feel more comfort-able in a place that fits with your basic personality.

An individual's self concept is the core of his personality.
It affects every aspect of human behaviour: the ability
to learn, the capacity to grow and change. A strong
positive self-image is the best possible preparation for
success in life.

Dr Joyce Brothers

Know thyself

A greater awareness of your preferred state of being will help you to understand why you may find some situations more anxiety-provoking than others. A noisy, crowded office with frequent meetings of large groups all shouting out at each other will create a sense of tension for an introvert, while an extrovert will thrive in a large noisy office, look forward to meetings where they can express themselves and get caught up in the energy of the interactions. The release of energy will help calm them down as their need for excitement and stimulation is satiated by the opportunities for self-expression. They, on the other hand, will not cope well with a job that leaves them on their own for long periods as they will quickly feel isolated and lose concentration.

If you want to get a general idea of your personality there are some tests and questionnaires you can access – you can find links to them in the glossary at the back of the book. The more you know about yourself, the better equipped you will be to make choices about which type of work would ideally complement your character. You will have many varied talents, skills and abilities. Your education and intellectual abilities will obviously have an influence on the range of work available to you, too. There is no point wanting to be a brain surgeon if you haven't already got a medical degree and are scared of blood.

REMEMBER THIS!!! If you can work in a job that suits your personality, you will feel more at ease. Just because you did particularly well in certain subjects at school and further education, it does not mean that you will be happiest choosing a career to match those areas of proficiency. If you are unhappy at work for an extended period of time it may be that there is a mismatch between your personality and the job.

In an ideal world, we would all be able to choose exactly the job that really suits us. The reality is that we often feel lucky just to have a job at all. It is okay to sometimes examine what is going on if we feel there is something wrong at work. People are often scared to even begin to admit to themselves that things aren't right. Take the bold step of really looking at what is going on. This will help reduce your confusion, which is the first step towards improving things.

The key points

- Feelings of anxiety and instability at work are natural

- Allow yourself to consider that you are feeling uncomfortable to begin to address problems and challenges at work

- Know your own personality to begin to address problems and challenges at work

- Your personality will influence what type of job will suit you, but does not mean you are unsuited to your current job

3. Anxiety at work

'I'm so worried I'm going to get this wrong.'

'I can't sleep for worrying about work.'

'I'm scared I won't be able to get this report out on time.'

Do these sort of comments sound familiar? Do you often experience similar concerns yourself? By their very nature working environments place a certain amount of pressure upon us; pressure to succeed, to meet deadlines, to avoid mistakes and to meet targets. It's not unusual to have a great many demands competing for our attention, all of which seem very important.

To a certain degree, feeling this kind of pressure is a good thing – it motivates us, encourages us to go the extra mile and gives us a sense of pride and achievement when we are able to meet the demands placed upon us. However, it is all too easy for responsible concern to tip over into real anxiety and panic which are not only horrible to experience on a personal level but also likely to impact upon your ability to work effectively. It's therefore important to spot when you have a problem and take steps to address it as quickly as possible.

Remember the fight or flight response? It is important to be prepared to deal with what you perceive as threats at work. As adrenaline is released into our bloodstream in response to a perceived threat we start to feel slightly on edge. We become more alert. This isn't necessarily a bad thing; I had a colleague who used to say that if he didn't feel a little nervous before giving a presentation, that in itself would worry him. He needed that edge to perform to his optimum.

But at some point increasing levels of adrenaline can escalate from concern to anxiety and, in extreme cases, to a panic attack.

Only you can recognize when healthy concern or nervousness have started to snowball into something more problematic. When you start to feel truly uncomfortable, that is when you can use the CBT Think Kit.

Stop, listen, look

- Stop when you start to feel uncomfortable.

- Listen to your body for signs that adrenaline levels are starting to rise.

- Look to identify what event or situation is triggering your response.

Using the Think Kit to tackle anxiety

We will now look at some case studies where CBT is used to help alleviate different kinds of work-related anxiety. After seeing how the Think Kit can be applied in these scenarios you will be far better equipped to use it in your own life to solve your own problems.

Louise

Louise is a graphic designer and has been given a new project to work on with a big new client. She very much wants to make a good impression but has found herself struggling with all the new responsibilities that the project entails. She is working every evening at home as well as at the weekends, in order to get everything ready for the deadline. She really wants the approval of her boss, her team and the client. She is also a perfectionist, and has a strong fear of failure. She has started to become withdrawn and has begun losing sleep.

Remember how the Think Kit works – ABC.

- Identify the situation – the **A**

- Spot the feelings that are present as a consequence – the **C**

- But in between **A** and **C** there must be a **B** – the belief. That's the 'should, ought or must' thinking that makes the situation cause the feeling.

The situation is that Louise has an important and demanding project to work on. As a result she is feeling anxious about not doing well enough. But what about her beliefs? What is she thinking? Use the words should, ought or must to help you frame her thoughts.

Here are a few ideas:

'I must do really well on this project, it would be terrible if I didn't. What will everyone think if I mess this up? Probably that I'm an idiot and not worthy of having these kinds of opportunity. I've known all along that I'm not very good and now they will find out. I could be demoted or even put on the redundancy list. I must work, work, work. I shouldn't go out or socialize because that is wasting time that could be better spent trying to improve my work'.

If Louise knew about the CBT Think Kit, she could use it to change this thinking and stop making herself so anxious that she is on the verge of a panic attack. She could adjust the very rigid beliefs she has about the situation and its potential consequences and replace them with less extreme, more helpful beliefs. She might say to herself:

'I would prefer to do well on this project, and I will give it my best shot. I will work steadily and carefully. I'll plan out what needs to be done, and include some leisure time so I have some balance in my life – wearing myself out is not going to help me work effectively. If I don't do an absolutely perfect report, I won't like it but I can accept it. How is making myself highly anxious, losing sleep and withdrawing helping me? It's not.'

Now let's consider another case.

Andy

Andy, 35, works for a PR firm. His appraisal with his line manager is due very soon and it is preying on his mind. He has not been sleeping well and has been feeling edgy at home. He snapped at his children several times recently. The first thing he does once the children are in bed is open a bottle of wine, give his wife one glass and then finish the rest himself. He wakes early, at around 3 or 4 am and arrives at work feeling tired and strained. His concentration is reduced and he has made a couple of mistakes recently, including inviting candidates for a new role to an interview when they had not been shortlisted.

You are probably becoming quite familiar with the Think Kit by now, and hopefully have been able to spot the following.

The actual situation (A) is Andy's upcoming appraisal.

As a consequence (C) Andy is feeling anxious and withdrawn.

And in basic terms the belief (B) that is causing the problem must be something like: 'I must do well in my appraisal.'

Andy's belief that he must do well in his appraisal is very strong. As long as he is thinking this way, he makes himself anxious; after all he has no way of knowing whether he is going to do well or not. In that sense, his worries are irrational. There may be things he could do to enhance his prospects of a favourable appraisal – maybe not. One thing is certain: the anxiety caused by his rigid belief is making him behave in ways that are definitely not helping.

Once again, in order to transform his overriding anxiety into a more healthy concern Andy needs to address his problematic beliefs.

Instead of thinking 'I *must* do well', Andy should think 'I would *prefer* to do well, but how is worrying so much helping me? I end up drinking too much because I think it helps me relax, I shout at my family and I don't sleep well because I am turning things over and over in my mind. I get so tired that I make mistakes at work which are exactly what might result in me getting a poor appraisal – it all becomes a vicious circle. I am going to try really hard to change the way I view the appraisal. I would *prefer* to do well in it, but if I don't it really isn't the end of the world. I won't like having a mediocre appraisal result but I can stand it. I will have a healthy concern but not make myself highly anxious.'

Now it's your turn. Think of a time when you were worrying about something at work.

Something that kept weighing heavily on your mind so that you became aware you were feeling anxious.

1.   What was the thing you were anxious about?

2.   How did it affect you? Feel free to refer back to page 27 to check some of the symptoms

3.   What were some of your behaviours at that time? Were they likely to improve the situation or make it worse?

Have a go at using the Think Kit.

•   Identify the A – the activating situation or event.

•   Then identify the C – the feelings and behaviours that have been triggered by A.

•   Finally try to work out what your beliefs were – the missing B.

•   How do you think you could have changed those beliefs to reduce the anxieties? The more helpful beliefs should have this kind of shape to them: 'I would have preferred that things weren't that way but the fact is they were. I could have changed the way I viewed things – although I didn't like it I could have accepted that life doesn't always go exactly as I would like. There is no point upsetting myself about something that I can't change.'

•   Change your rigid beliefs to preferences in this way then you will be able to accept things and move on.

Fear and serious anxiety

Fear is closely allied to anxiety, and when you are feeling anxious it can be very easy to work yourself up into being actively afraid. There are different degrees of worrying with fear towards the more serious end of the scale. If you start to genuinely fear something and do not address this problem it can have severe consequences, such as panic attacks, the development of a phobia, post-traumatic stress disorder and, for some people, obsessive compulsive disorders.

We all experience things differently and people may be physically and mentally affected by the same circumstance to varying degrees. Some people may say they are 'born worriers', and there can be some truth in that – it has been found that some people are more susceptible to perceived threats in their environment and their arousal levels may peak much quicker than those of others.

A company which was having financial difficulties announced to its employees that to cut overheads there would have to be some redundancies. They were told that the list of people they would need to discuss this with would be emailed at close of business that Friday. Two employees received the email at the same time. One of them, Jo, became very agitated and started hyperventilating at her desk. Ian, on the other hand, was not so adversely affected; he remained calm and was even able to comfort Jo when he noticed her distress.

It's not at all difficult to imagine a scenario such as this, is it? The fact is that some of us are more affected by perceived threats than others. Studies of identical twins have shown that they have similar stress responses in similar situations and this has led to further research that shows that anxiety responses are in part genetic. There is a gene known as the serotonin transfer gene which appears to have a connection to the manifestation of anxiety disorders. And of course our previous experiences also influence how we respond to challenging circumstances.

If you are one of those people who tends to worry more than others it can be hard, especially if people around you seem consistently calm and unflustered. Unfortunately there is no magic way to turn you into a naturally less-concerned person, but this is not to say that you cannot do a lot to tackle these problematic feelings – the CBT Think Kit can still work for you, it just may take a bit more effort and practice to bring those anxiety levels down.

REMEMBER THIS!!! If you find yourself really crippled by severe anxiety, fear or phobias which the strategies in this book are unable to help you with, don't suffer in silence. If you seek help from a medical professional they will be able to give you advice on the range of options available to help tackle the problem.

More strategies for coping with anxiety

CBT is not going to make you into a consistently calm, unstressed person who sails through life without a single hitch. Of course you will get anxious sometimes. The CBT Think Kit will help you work through unhelpful thinking so that fewer things make you anxious, but you also need to be able to use other methods too to bring those anxiety levels down on those unavoidable occasions when they do rear their head. There are plenty of anxiety-reducing techniques and routines that you can incorporate into your life. Here are some practical things you could try.

- Make a list of all the things you are anxious about. Keep a 'thought diary' and look for the things that wind you up the most. You will then be more aware of potentially difficult situations for you, and can take steps to prepare yourself using the Think Kit.

- Make a playlist of your favourite music to listen to when you are feeling worried – it can help to soothe the savage beast!

- Have a mantra that you say to yourself when you start to feel anxious or recognize that your adrenaline levels are rising. It can be something as simple as, 'I do not need to make myself anxious', or can be more personal to you.

- Focus on the feelings, accept that it is natural to feel some anxiety and then consciously decide that you will not allow them to spiral out of control.

- Be aware of your breathing and try to keep it slow and regular.

- Leave your desk if you can, in order to get away from whatever it is that you are anxious about. Perhaps go outside for a walk at lunchtime, preferably on your own.

- Actors frequently employ the technique of lifting their shoulders up to their ears for a few 'shrugs', gently at first then more vigorously to loosen up and relieve tension. Try this technique yourself.

How are you doing so far?

You have now had quite a few examples of how to apply the CBT Think Kit to problems. They have been quite repetitive on purpose. The more often you go over the Think Kit, the more it will sink in. We have talked here about anxiety in general but it can be linked with many other emotions, such as anger or guilt. In the next chapters we will look at applying CBT to other common problems that can arise at work. Don't worry if you still find the idea of changing your rigid beliefs difficult – like anything else it takes time to learn. The more you read through the examples in this book the more dealing with problems in this way will become second nature.

The key points

- Workplaces by their very nature put pressure on us

- Pressure can be positive: it can motivate and encourage us to achieve better results

- Pressure can also cause anxiety and it is important to recognise and tackle this before it gets worse

- Recognise when feelings of anxiety begin, and challenge those negative beliefs

- Use your CBT Think Kit to think more positively about a situation and so create a more positive consequence

4. Anger and frustration at work

'This is the last straw.'

'You had your chance, now you've blown it.'

'Oh no, I've messed up again, I can't get even the simplest thing right.'

'How dare you speak to me like that.'

Whoa! Easy tiger! There seems to be a lot of tension around those comments doesn't there?

Do you find yourself getting angry quite frequently at work? Or maybe just sometimes but with very serious consequences? It is normal to experience a certain amount of anger at everyday annoyances at work, but when it goes too far or you are not in control, it becomes a problem. You can think of it on a sliding scale, ranging from mild irritation, through to frustration, annoyance and on towards full blown anger.

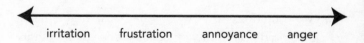

irritation   frustration   annoyance   anger

CBT can help you to bring that level down by questioning the beliefs that are causing the anger and replacing them with more helpful ones. It can also help you to recognize an increasing level of anger and halt it before it becomes a real problem or you upset yourself. It is natural, for example, to react with a flash of negative emotion when you find yourself on the receiving end of someone else's anger. It's all too easy to allow that to tip you over into full blown anger, but using CBT strategies you can get a handle on your own emotions and start to calm down.

 Try this exercise. Think of three times when you have felt angry about work and write them down. Look at them in turn and for each one consider what it was about the situation that made you feel angry. When you think about it, do you still get upsetting feelings? If the answer is 'yes', you can safely assume that those issues have still not been resolved for you. Another great thing about using CBT is that it can help you go over past events and work on them in the present, so you really do move on.

If you always do what you always did, you will always get what you always got.

Whatever attitudes and views you had at the time, it was by holding rigidly on to them that you made yourself angry.

Different types of anger

There are different types of anger, and each of us may be more prone to some types than others. It's worth thinking about what kind of anger you feel most often, and how this might affect your life, both at work and in general.

Anger at yourself

Do you get angry at yourself? When you make mistakes do you get upset and berate yourself? We can often be our own worst critics. Some of us treat ourselves in a way we would not dream of treating others.

When you get angry at yourself, you can use the CBT Think Kit in exactly the same way that you would when struggling with anger directed at external targets. You need to identify what it is that you are winding yourself up about. However, this time the trigger is not an external situation or another person. It is your inner self-talk. Once you've identified the trigger, you need to find the 'should, ought or must' demands that you are placing on yourself. You may be the type of person who strives for perfection and anything short of that fills you with feelings of anger at yourself. You can use the same techniques that we discussed to help stem the rising tide of anxiety (see page 24) to help stop anger levels rising. When you recognize that you are starting to feel angry, accept what is happening and apply your 'stop' strategy. I use the mantra 'I do not need to make myself angry' – very simple, perhaps, but repeating it to myself helps me focus on the feelings. It gives me a breathing space to recognize the 'should, ought or must' thinking and not let the anger escalate.

Anger at others

Rather than inward-facing anger at yourself, you may find yourself frequently getting angry at others and having outbursts of verbal or even physical aggression. Certainly the latter is always completely unacceptable. But even in the case of the former, while it may feel good to voice your anger you will probably find that in the long term this causes you problems. If you were a manager in a position to promote someone in your team, would you be likely to go for the angry colleague or the one who challenges others in a calm and considered manner? CBT can help you decide to adopt a 'conscious compliant' attitude, that is, you think through your behavioural options and realize that although you may not like the situation, in the long run, you are more likely to achieve your goals by avoiding anger. This is not to say that you abandon all your principles and become an emotionless automaton, but you make a conscious choice about how and when to express your feelings

Anger at the world

Remember in the first chapter we looked at three categories of negative thoughts, including negative thoughts towards the world? It is this generalized frustration at the world that we are expressing when we say things like 'It's not fair.' There can be much injustice, inequality and unfairness in the workplace too. When something is completely outside your control then obviously the only thing that this anger does is compound your unhappiness.

Can I use CBT to stop me feeling angry about the past?

Holding negative thoughts in your head from the past can be the trigger for present day anger. The same kind of thinking patterns may be responsible for you feeling angry in different situations. It can therefore be highly beneficial to analyze past difficulties. You can use CBT retrospectively to change the way you view events in the past and to move on.

You will have to practise it until you really *feel* differently because you have changed the way you view those past events. Let's imagine that in a previous job you were passed over for promotion in favour of someone with less experience. You had hit all your sales targets while they had not, and they were consistently late in to the office while you were always on time. However, they were friendly with several members of the management team and used to go out to the pub with them. You are convinced that this is the only reason they got the position instead of you, which is very unjust.

Now, whilst all of this may be fact, CBT would encourage you to ask yourself, 'How is it helping me today to keep upsetting myself about the past?' As an adult you have choices. You can continue to hold those beliefs – 'I should have been given the promotion' – or you can change your view to, 'I would have preferred to have been given the promotion but the fact is I wasn't. It was tough but I can accept it.' By changing how you view past events you can change how you feel about them today. No one is asking you to like it, but it is more healthy to move on.

In time, anger can subside; you may still feel annoyed about whatever caused it but it doesn't intrude on your waking day so much. CBT can help you go through this process much more quickly, so that you do not spend weeks, months and even years simmering away with resentment about something. It is not healthy for you to hold grudges. That drip drip of adrenaline when you trigger your anger response is wear and tear on your body.

And although it may be harder than dealing with anger from your past, the same also applies to tackling anger in the moment it first happens. In the heat of the moment it may be difficult to spot your problematic beliefs and confront them, but with practice you can learn to do this. Not only is this beneficial from the point of view of your own well-being; it will also make you a better communicator and therefore a better colleague.

 Think about your colleagues at work. Do some of them tend to show more outward anger or aggression at times than others? And do the angrier ones make for better company or get better results from the team?

Anger produces negative reactions in others. Of course it is important to make your views known, but how you do this is crucial. A good piece of advice is not to give your opinions when you are fired up and angry. When you are emotionally charged people will perceive you as a threat. People who rant and rail may often regret not what they said, but how they said it. CBT can be used to bring the angry emotions down to a calmer level, before you challenge the decisions of others and give your own opinions. Visualize yourself being angry – is this how you prefer to be? Surely not. If you want to be listened to, you need to take the threats out of your body language.

What happens when you are angry?

Anger has a strong effect on our bodies. It is the fight or flight response again (see page 30). The angrier you become, the more adrenaline is pumped into your bloodstream. It is possible for the level to rise so much that rational thinking is almost impossible as your body is concentrating its efforts on maximizing its physical strength in order to deal with a perceived threat. After all, thinking wouldn't have been much good to our ancestors in threat situations: there is no point standing and philosophizing on the ethics of a bear wanting to eat you when your best choice of survival is to run.

However, such an extreme physical response is rarely helpful to us nowadays in the modern world. The graph opposite shows that there is a point at which you perform your best when you are 'fired up'. If you go beyond that point then your mental functioning is impaired. The

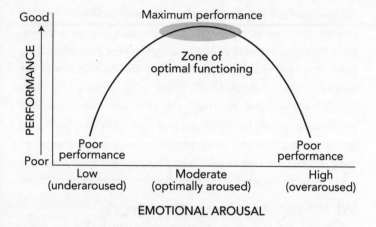

Good | Maximum performance

Zone of
optimal functioning

PERFORMANCE

Poor
performance

Poor
performance

Poor

Low
(underaroused)

Moderate
(optimally aroused)

High
(overaroused)

EMOTIONAL AROUSAL

rising curve is reflective of the amount of adrenaline being poured into the body, which is frequently due to anger or anxiety. Keeping a handle on your anger by being careful to examine the beliefs which are causing it can stop you from ending up in the 'danger zone' of over-arousal and poor performance.

Over-thinking

Angry feelings have a common thread, like all the issues that we have looked at in this book: they arise from your thinking. When you start to think about something which you are uncomfortable about – say, for example, having to give a presentation to a large group of people at work – then it will be on your mind. Since it's an uncomfortable thought, you may try to push it away. However, it is still there lurking in the background and will continue to make you feel tense. The constant dripping of adrenaline into your body, will start giving you flutters of anxiety symptoms. Your general levels of alertness will be raised as your body perceives a potential threat.

For a while this may be beneficial, but it will not take much to push you from alertness and anxiety over into full-blown anger. You may, for example, find that someone has used your coffee mug and suddenly you are very angry. A seemingly minor and unrelated trigger in the environment can send that extra drip of adrenaline into the already bubbling reservoir. This will tip the balance from generalized anxiety into full-blown flight or fight response that easily explodes into anger. This could express itself in any number of different ways, none of which are likely to benefit either yourself or others around you. CBT can help you be more aware of your levels of frustration as they start rising to intervene before you tip over from irritation into anger.

Noreen

Noreen, 52, is a team manager in a call centre that deals with emergency home heating problems. She has twenty people in her team and they are set hourly quality control targets. Noreen is constantly under pressure to keep her team focused and has to keep a lid on her own frustrations until she gets home from work. Often she starts shouting at her family as soon as she comes in for not tidying the house or sorting dinner out. She constantly finds fault with her husband, and calls him a 'useless man'. She has even been known to throw plates at him in the kitchen or seek him out in his den and slam his laptop shut while he is playing computer games.

Let's try running Noreen's situation through the Think Kit.

- Identify the situation – the A

- Spot the feelings or behaviour that arise as a consequence – the C

- Spot the missing belief (B) that comes between them – the 'should, ought or must' thinking

The situation is that Noreen is in a high-pressure job that doesn't seem to allow her much time to blow off steam herself during the day.

Noreen's main feelings appear to be frustration tipping over into anger.

What about the all-important beliefs? What might she be thinking? As usual, it may be helpful to use the words should, ought or must to frame the thoughts:

'I must _____.'
'I should _____.'
'I ought _____.'

Perhaps Noreen's thinking is going something like this: 'The team must hit their targets; if they don't it will look like I can't manage them and I will appear incompetent. They should be more efficient at answering calls – some of them spend far too long talking to the callers and passing the time of day with them when they should just be getting their details and moving on. I have so much to do and the family should really be helping me and sorting the house out considering how hard I work. My husband ought to get them organized – I have to do everything myself. He shouldn't lock himself away with the computer. I'm really fed up with it all and I am entitled to give them all a piece of my mind.'

If Noreen could change her thinking so she didn't place so many demands on her team, her family and herself, she could limit her feelings of frustration. They are natural and understandable in response to her situation, but can be capped so that they don't escalate into the rising tensions which build up and erupt as anger. She needs to look at each of her beliefs in turn and test their validity. For example, is it really true that if her team doesn't hit its targets once or twice, people will think she is incompetent? Certainly it would be better if the team hit the targets, and it might not reflect brilliantly on her if they fail to do so consistently, but the sudden jump to people thinking she must be incompetent is an extreme one. Would she judge another manager in this way? Probably not.

Equally she needs to realize that there is only so much control that she can assert over the people in her life – clinging to the belief that people *should* behave in a certain way when clearly they do not will only make her angry; it will not change the situation itself. Having identified the unhelpful beliefs, she could then see why it would be more rational for her to 'prefer' that her team and family faced up to their responsibilities. She could accept that they have their own limitations and remind herself that shouting at them doesn't help anyone, least of all her. This is not to say that she needs to allow either her team or her family to behave in whatever way they like, simply that she needs to control her emotions so that she does not upset herself and is able to challenge the behaviour of others in a calm and constructive way when appropriate. You will see in the next case study that it can be helpful to have a strategy already in place for when you can feel the tensions mounting to stop the spill over into anger.

Chris

Chris, a diversity trainer, joined a business networking group. At each monthly meeting, one business was given the opportunity to present to the group in order to advertise their services. One month, the local hospice organization was going to present. When Chris arrived the charity's director, Ruth, had set up display boards with information and was ready to give her talk. The chairman of the networking group always did an introduction at the start of each meeting. That week, before Ruth began her presentation, the chairman told a couple of jokes and made some comments about women which seemed blatantly sexist. Chris was livid, he felt his face reddening and his pulse rising.

Your turn again now, apply the CBT Think Kit to Chris's feelings of anger

- Identify the situation – the A.

- Spot the feelings or behaviour that arise as a consequence – the C.

- Spot the missing belief (B) that comes between them – the 'should, ought or must' thinking.

Chris's thinking might be something along the lines of: 'The chairman of the group should not make jokes like these. It is terrible that he would make such sexist remarks, and equally terrible that some of the group laughed at them. Here is a woman who has come to tell us about the wonderful work the hospice does, and here is the chairman making fun of women.'

A summary of the core belief Chris holds here might be something like: 'People should not be disrespectful and ridicule others.' However strongly he may feel about this, and however much we might all agree with the sentiment, by holding on to such a rigid belief in that moment all he is doing is making himself angry.'

It's obvious that this belief is not going to change the way people like the chairman behave or make the situation better; all it will do is continue to upset Chris. Knowing this, he could change his thinking to 'I would prefer that people did not make sexist and disrespectful remarks, but the fact is, sometimes they do. I can stand it. I don't like it but how is winding myself up into a frenzy helping the woman who is about to do the presentation, or helping me? If I jump up now and object to the chairman's remarks it will disrupt the meeting and people will feel uncomfortable. It would be better to confront this issue later, calmly and rationally – if I do that the chances of the problem being dealt with successfully are also higher.'

Chris has plenty of choices about how to pursue the matter afterwards – he could speak to the chairman personally to express his disappointment, or write to the secretary of the group to put forward his opinions, or even choose not to attend any more meetings. Whatever he might decide, it is better to make that decision when he is calm and thinking clearly. Controlling your anger does not mean being weak or 'rolling over' to other people – it means looking out for your own well being and giving yourself the space to ensure that you make the best choices.

Now try applying the same process to your own anger. Think of a time when you felt angry at or about work. What was the thing you were angry about? How did it affect you? What were some of your feelings and behaviours at the time?

Use the Think Kit:

- Identify the situation – the A.

- Spot the feelings or behaviour that arise as a consequence – the C.

- Spot the missing belief (B) that comes between them – the 'should, ought or must' thinking.

- How do you think you could have changed your beliefs at that time to reduce the anxieties?

Okay, have a rest now. Your brain needs time to assimilate what you have learned so far. Therapy sessions are usually not more than once a week. There is a reason for this. Most of the real work goes on between the sessions, as you reflect and think about how to apply what you have learned to your own life. And when trying to replace your own problematic, rigid beliefs with more helpful ones, don't be too hard on yourself if you don't seem to be getting great results to begin with. Our beliefs often become habits that are hard to change; doing so takes awareness, practice and above all, time.

The key points

- Understand that anger is a common, natural reaction

- Identify the type of anger you feel in order to begin to address it

- Identify the trigger for your anger and the 'should, ought or must' demands

- Apply your 'stop' strategy when you feel yourself getting angry

- Adopt a 'conscious compliant' attitude: think through your behavioural options and recognize you will achieve more by not getting angry

- Be aware of rising frustration before it turns into anger

- With practice you can spot your problematic beliefs and confront them, even in the heat of the moment

5. CBT for guilt at work

'I feel awful that I forgot to put that advert in the paper as I was meant to.'

'I made completely the wrong decision about stocking that merchandise.'

'I feel I've let everyone down by being off sick and missing the conference.'

Why do we feel guilty?

Guilt comes about when we feel we fall short of our own expectations. We all have our own standards and if we fail to meet them, we can start to dwell on what we perceive as our shortcomings. In this kind of situation you will probably find that you end up berating yourself – 'I have done something wrong. If people knew what I have done they would not want to associate with me. No one must know what I have done. I am a bad person.' Feelings of guilt and shame may result in a person keeping what they have done to themselves. This usually only serves to perpetuate the thinking, leading to further upset.

 Think of a time when you made a mistake at work and felt guilty about it. Did you tell anyone what had happened? Try to remember how long you felt guilty for – perhaps you even feel guilty thinking about it today.

If a good friend of yours had done the same thing, how would you view them? Would it make you think badly of them? The chances are that you would see that they made a mistake and think it unfortunate but that wouldn't colour your opinion of them as a person or stop them being your friend. It's easy to have tougher and more rigid beliefs about ourselves than about others. But being hard on yourself is not healthy, particularly over a length of time. CBT can help you rationalize guilty feelings so that you are able to move on.

Anyone who has never made a mistake has never tried anything new.

Albert Einstein

You and your behaviour are not the same thing. Making a mistake does not mean you are generally incompetent or a bad person. We all make mistakes – it's unfortunate but how is continually upsetting yourself helping you? You wouldn't condemn your friend so why be so hard on yourself?

CBT does not encourage you to have no concern or regret for mistakes. It is healthy and appropriate to feel regret when, looking back, you wish you had acted in a different way. But when this tips into overriding guilt, it can be unhealthy. In fact studies show that feeling prolonged guilt can lower your immune levels in your body. Once again the correct emotional response comes somewhere on a sliding scale. You need to have appropriate concerns about your own behaviour and an ability to cope with responsibilities, but not be crippled by excessive, unhelpful guilt.

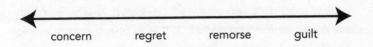

concern   regret   remorse   guilt

Triggers for guilt

Often it is the most caring, considerate and responsible people who are most prone to guilt. That's the irony; if you don't care about others in the first place then you are unlikely to feel as much guilt. That is not to say that CBT encourages you to be selfish in a negative way, but sometimes the balance between putting your own needs and wants second to those of others could mean that you are constantly in a state of tension trying to please. Maybe you could learn how to be your own best friend first sometimes.

Think about developing 'enlightened self-interest', where you weigh up if the way you are behaving is good for you in the long run, and allow yourself to look at other options if it is not. Sometimes we make it hard for ourselves by going over our mistakes again and again. You can worry too much about if you have upset someone else, if you could have done better, or if you are a good person.

A little of what you fancy does you good

A study by a team at the University of Hull, including Dr Geoff Lowe, showed that guilt can actually make you ill.

Researchers found that people who felt guilty about their 'life's little pleasures' – such as eating chocolate, having a lie-in or (the pleasure that scored the highest for guilt inducement) watching soaps on television – in general had less effective immune systems. It was found that thinking about how they shouldn't do these things lowered the subject's levels of immunoglobulin A, which is an antibody secreted to combat infection. The people who worried like this were more likely to suffer colds, stomach upsets, coughs and other minor infections.

Of course this kind of guilt at indulging oneself is slightly different to the guilt we might have for, say, failing to hit an important deadline for our boss. In the one case we are guilty about something we have deliberately done and in the other for failing to do something properly. However, the root cause of the guilt is the same in both instances: we have not measured up against our own beliefs about how we should behave. Using the Think Kit you can stop concern about mistakes and other issues spiralling down into unhelpful and upsetting guilt. No one else makes you feel guilty, you do that all by yourself.

THINK ABOUT IT

How is feeling guilty helping me?

You know the answer by now: it doesn't.

Beware the tyranny of 'shoulds'

This is an important point, relevant to any of the upsetting feelings you experience when applying the Think Kit, though it is particularly likely to crop up with the issue of guilt. We often have rigid and unhelpful beliefs about guilt itself – that we *should* feel guilty about some things. You can even wind yourself up into thinking that you are a bad person if you don't feel guilty about something, and become guilty about not being guilty! This is called a secondary emotional disturbance and we will see it come up in the second case study in this chapter. If you experience this kind of problem it has to be tackled first before you look at other issues. The balance between a healthy sense of concern and an overriding feeling of guilt is down to you. You can help yourself to stop the slide from concern to guilt.

> *If there were nothing wrong in the world, there wouldn't be anything for us to do.*
>
> George Bernard Shaw

Albert Ellis, the founder of CBT, placed a lot of emphasis on the fact that 'we are all fallible human beings'. We all make mistakes. We don't intend to make mistakes, but sometimes 'stuff happens'. That is the important point, we don't *intend* to mess up. At the same time we need to make sure we do not catastrophize our mistakes, thinking they are more serious than they really are – we need to get them in perspective.

TRY IT NOW! Here is a timeline exercise to use the next time you start feeling guilty about something at work. It's very simple. Take the issue about which you are feeling guilty and run through the following questions, thinking about each one in as much detail as possible:

- How important do you think the thing you feel guilty about will be by the end of next week?

- What impact will it still be having in a month's time?

- How about in a year's time?

If you answer these questions in an honest, objective way you will almost certainly see that the issue is not as big as you managed to convince yourself it was. Using the time line exercise can help you get the problem in perspective. Having a sleepless night obsessing about your error of judgement, or letting thoughts about the carelessness of your behaviour go round and round in your head is not going to either change the mistake or help you work effectively the next day. One of my professors used to say he thought human beings had a genetic tendency to think irrationally. It certainly does seem to be the case that our default mode is to think in ways that aren't helpful to us.

Struggles with guilt at work

If you are in a job which gives you the time and opportunity to work in the ways that suit you, you will have a good chance of feeling fulfilled – job done! However, we don't live in a perfect world and almost all of us will have times at work when the pressure mounts and we get stressed. We may feel that we cannot do the job in exactly the way we would wish to, or to our very best standards. This can create tension.

When there is a mismatch between what we are thinking and how we are behaving in this way it is called **cognitive dissonance**. An example might be throwing your newspaper out in the general rubbish because the paper recycling bin that is usually nearby appears to have been moved. In fact you may feel quite strongly that you want to recycle but because you are on a tight deadline you don't have time to run round looking for the new location of the bin. Your behaviour does not match your beliefs. This would probably only be a minor thing for most people, but it could still make you feel slightly guilty.

And you may find yourself running into situations which cause much more serious cognitive dissonance. After all, there is usually quite a lot at stake when you are working – on the one hand you want to do the best job you can for the company, but on the other you have your personal moral code and standards to consider. When these two clash we can be left feeling extremely uncomfortable.

Katharine

Katharine had been asked to be on the interview panel for an internal promotion. She was a departmental manager and the vacancy had arisen in a different department, where her friend Mark worked. There were six applicants for the post, including Mark. After the interviews, the panel of interviewers (Katharine and two others) met to discuss who they would appoint. One of the applicants in particular had an outstanding record and, despite having only been with the company for six months, was obviously the most suitable applicant. She was duly appointed and the other candidates were told that they had been unsuccessful. Katharine felt terrible. She didn't know how she was going to face Mark. She felt guilty that he hadn't been appointed and thought he would be angry with her. She avoided her friend for a week and had sleepless nights worrying about it.

Katharine's situation is a clear case of cognitive dissonance. Let's apply the Think Kit. The actual situation (A) that has caused the issue is obviously that Mark was not the best candidate, and as a result was not given the job. The consequence (C) is that Katharine feels guilty. She held the belief (B) that you ought always to support your friends, but this conflicted with strong beliefs about fairness and professionalism which won out and caused her to support the stronger candidate. As a result her behaviour ended up being in conflict with her belief about friendship, causing cognitive dissonance.

Katharine knows that really she has made the right decision – she would probably feel a lot guiltier if she had blindly supported Mark in spite of the fact that he was not the most suitable person for the job. Knowing this, she could seek to change her demand on herself that she *should* have appointed him to a *preference* that she would have liked to appoint him had it been possible. Unfortunately he was not the best candidate so it was not – that's just the way things were. She is a little sad about this but nevertheless if she lost his approval as a result she would have to accept that.

In fact Mark was more upset that Katharine had avoided him for a week than at not getting the post. He said that he hadn't expected to get the job but enjoyed the interview and considered it good experience for the future.

A problem shared ...

When we feel guilty about a mistake we have made at work we often instinctively keep it to ourselves, trying to delay the inevitable moment when a colleague or manager discovers it. While this is perhaps understandable it only serves to make us feel guiltier. A mistake is also more likely to be forgiven if you admit it straight away so that it can be dealt with.

Visualize making a mistake at work or, if you can, think about a real mistake that is bothering you right now. You have two choices as to how you can deal with it. Either you say nothing and hope that it will somehow pass unnoticed or you 'confess all'.

If you choose to say nothing, what might the consequences be? Take yourself through the possible stages of what could happen. How might you feel?

If, on the other hand, you choose to tell someone, what might be the consequences? The idea of confronting the issue and owning up may be extremely uncomfortable, but ask yourself this: what is the worst thing that could happen? Be objective about this. Don't catastrophize. If you can honestly consider the worst-case scenario – which is usually a lot better than you might have worked yourself up to believe – it can take the fear out of the situation.

Make a chart to show:

Advantages of saying nothing/Disadvantages of saying nothing

Advantages of reporting the mistake/Disadvantages of reporting the mistake

By writing down this cost-benefit analysis, you can help yourself rationalize the situation and see things as they really are. Writing down concerns helps you to get things in perspective, while just allowing the thoughts and feelings to run rampant in your head increases your anxiety and feelings of guilt. You can't change what happened, but you can change the way you view it. This can lead you on to new, constructive behaviour which will likely help you to limit any negative consequences arising from the original mistake.

Learn from your mistakes and use that knowledge to help you avoid repeating them in the future.

Mistakes and management

Letting people know when you have made a mistake is also a helpful management strategy. In research published in 2011 Larry Elkin concluded that managers who could admit when they had made a mistake were better liked by their teams. Obviously there is a limit to the number of mistakes that one can make in this context, as there is a point at which natural and humanizing fallibility changes into incompetence. But being able to show your human side now and then is no bad thing; you won't be condemned for all time.

Even a mistake may turn out to be the one thing necessary to a worthwhile achievement.

Henry Ford

CASE STUDY

Sanjeep

Sanjeep was a fire-fighter in a busy city. His job was physically challenging and also required him to use his problem-solving skills and initiative to resolve issues quickly and calmly. He could be called upon to fight fires and rescue people from burning buildings or to attend road traffic accidents and other emergencies. He loved his job and he felt he was really using his strengths to do something valuable and useful.

Just recently, however, an incident had been playing on his mind. He had been feeling guilty that a traffic jam in the city had slowed down their response time attending a community centre which was on fire. Although no one was hurt the devastation to the building meant that it could not be repaired and would have to be bulldozed. He knew that it had been a thriving centre and many older residents in the area had relied on it, using the daily programmes to keep active and sociable. He felt guilty that he and the rest of the team had not got there sooner.

Remember, **ABC:**

Actual Situation
Belief
Consequence

The actual situation (A) is the delay in getting to the fire. As a consequence (C) Sanjeep is feeling guilty. But what is the missing belief (B) which is causing the situation to result in this consequence?

What is his belief?

'I **must** _____.'
'I **should** _____.'
'I **ought** _____.'

Something like 'I should have got there sooner,' probably frames his belief pretty well.

As long as he holds on to the belief that he should have got there sooner, he will continue to feel guilty. If he can change his belief to something along the lines of 'I would have preferred that we had got there sooner, but unfortunately the traffic jam held us up. That wasn't my fault and I did everything in my power to get there as soon as possible. I regret that our response time was delayed, but I am not helping myself or the community centre by feeling guilty.' Once Sanjeep has reduced his feelings to a more healthy concern, he will be able to think more clearly – this might allow him to consider practical ways in which he could help the community centre. You can use the Think Kit in exactly the same way to deal with your own guilt.

REMEMBER THIS!!!

When you are thinking clearly and calmly, you allow yourself to be creative. You are more likely to come up with constructive new ways of behaving when your mind is not tied up with worries.

Emotionally demanding jobs

Some jobs put people in particularly stressful or upsetting situations. Jobs of this kind might include working in the police, fire brigade, ambulance service, coastguard, armed services or in medical professions. Being exposed to situations where human lives hang in the balance can be very difficult to cope with, and if something tragic happens which a person somehow perceives as their fault, the guilt they experience can be extreme. A specialized form of CBT, called Post Traumatic Stress Disorder Therapy is often appropriate in such cases. The usual warning signs associated with emotional distress which we considered earlier (page 27) may well manifest themselves, and additionally the person may experience some of the following:

- extreme guilt
- nightmares
- flashbacks
- feelings of isolation
- irritability
- avoiding reminders of the incident
- depression

- alcohol or drug misuse
- insomnia

These symptoms may occur a matter of days or weeks after the incident, but can also take much longer to appear. There could be a gap of months or even years before the effects begin to manifest. It is important not to ignore the symptoms. They can come and go, so often people do not realize that the difficulties they are experiencing are connected to the traumatic incident or the effects of working in a high-stress environment over time. Colleagues and family may notice these changes. In such situations it is very hard for a person to help themselves or to be helped by someone in their personal life, so seeking professional help is always advisable. Talking to a doctor is often the best first point of contact.

Guilty feelings can also be triggered in the workplace if we are left unaffected by negative occurrences that other people have to endure – if we survive a round of redundancies, escape a list of early retirement recommendations or are left out of a pay freeze when colleagues are put on one, for example.

Even outside relatively serious situations like this it is common for people to feel uncomfortable following a traumatic work occurrence that they have escaped relatively unscathed, and at such times it is important to differentiate between a healthy human empathy for others and unnecessary guilt.

Don't carry round a personal cloud of doom and damnation – by analyzing your beliefs and rationalizing the situation you can dissipate that cloud, learn from your experiences and move on. You and your behaviour are not the same thing. You can still be a basically good person, with high moral standards, but sometimes behave in ways that you are not proud of. Change your thinking and you have a better chance of behaving in more self-acceptable ways in the future.

> *Guilt is the source of sorrow 'tis the fiend,*
> *The avenging fiend,*
> *That follows us behind,*
> *With whips and stings.*

Nicholas Rowel

The key points

- Understand why you feel guilty and how to be less hard on yourself

- Develop 'enlightened self-interest': recognizing when to put your own needs above that of others is not selfish

- 'Cognitive dissonance' can cause problems in your working life

- Analyze and rationalize the negative beliefs that cause guilty feelings in order to move on and learn from your mistakes

- Put things in perspective: 'stuff happens'

6. Depression at work

'I don't think I can cope any more, this job is really getting on top of me.'

'I feel useless, I am always getting things wrong.'

'I dread going to work, I used to really like it but now I feel ill most of the time'

What is depression?

Depression is when a person experiences a state of low mood for a prolonged length of time. It isn't just a psychological condition but a physical one too. It isn't that you simply have a bad day, or feel a bit anti-social one weekend – it is an illness that can last for months or even years.

Some people have regular depressive episodes all their life, from puberty onwards. Others may just experience one or two instances where 'the black dog' descends and takes over their life. The important thing is to acknowledge that sometimes this may happen and when it does you need to accept that it is a serious condition and get some help. There are also strategies that you can put in place in order to prevent a difficult situation or period in your life from tipping you over into a full blown depressive episode.

How do you know if you are depressed? It is natural to feel a bit low or fed up about life now and then. In fact you would be pretty unique if you didn't feel low in spirits some days. But if these feelings persist over a few weeks, and you can't seem to shake them off, or if you start to find it hard to get out of bed because you dread having to get through the day, these could be warning signs that you are sliding into depression.

Depression is a condition that is on the increase in many countries. The World Health Organisation predicts that by 2030 it will be the main illness in the western world. The good news is that CBT has been found to be very helpful in alleviating depression. If you can recognize when you are showing some of the common symptoms, you can put strategies in place yourself which can help stop you declining to the point where clinical intervention may be necessary.

Depression can creep up on you. It is also a topic that still isn't really talked about too much. People can still feel some shame if they suffer from it and are often embarrassed to ask for information and seek help. There is no need to feel this way – depression is a very common and very treatable condition so anyone suffering from it should know two things: you are not alone and there is lots of help available.

Causes of depression

There does not seem to be one single cause of depression – it is often a combination of factors that impact upon a person. However, it does seem to appear to run in families, so there may be a genetic element. It is also known that a certain type of depression called Seasonal Affective Disorder (SAD) is caused by a reduction in the level of a hormone called serotonin in the body. When the sunlight decreases during winter, the bodies of sufferers react by producing less of this chemical. This has a direct effect on their body chemistry and they become depressed.

This shows a direct link between body and mind – depression is due to chemical changes in the body. Some people may have regular depressive episodes and this could be a lifelong battle for them. In this chapter, I will highlight some of the work situations that can contribute to depression. As ever, it is important to let your doctor know how you have been feeling as there may be other physical causes which need to be looked at.

The environment we are living and working in may be a factor in precipitating depression, as can events in our lives. In 1967 Thomas Homes and Richard Rahe put together a list of 43 stressful life events, the accumulation of several of which might be enough to push a person over into depression and ill health. Their list includes:

House buying and moving
End of a relationship – separation/divorce
Problems at work
Change in nature of work
Change of job
Redundancy
Unemployment
Retirement
Financial difficulties
Pregnancy

Birth of a baby
Death of a close relative

Events like these may not, on their own, have enough of an impact to cause real problems. However, when they start to stack up together they can make you more vulnerable to the changes in your body chemistry that can lead you into depression.

For example, in practice I have found that for working parents an extremely stressful time can be when you have young pre-school children. Their sleep patterns may vary each night and disturb the whole house. Continued sleep deprivation combined with the usual stresses of work (which ordinarily a person might be able to cope with) can be enough to cause a real problem. When your life feels as though one thing after another is demanding your attention, whether at home or at work, be sure to pay attention to your physical and mental state so that you do not push yourself too far.

The four areas of disruption

Depression can involve different aspects, including changes in mood, thinking, behaviour and physical health. Let's look briefly at each of these four in turn.

1. Mood changes

A person may feel numb or sad for long periods. They may also suffer from increased anxiety and irritability. Feelings of low self-worth and hopelessness are not uncommon. Symptoms may also include feeling tired all the time, even though they are sleeping a lot, or else going through a period of insomnia. They may find it hard to concentrate, feel frequently on edge, or feel worthless or stupid.

In extreme cases a person may decide that they can't go on feeling the way they do and may consider harming themselves to make the feelings stop. It is really important if you are having suicidal thoughts that you tell someone. If you feel you can't tell family or friends because you are ashamed or don't want to put this 'burden' on them, then do tell your doctor or ring a helpline for some support. There are help lines available 24 hours a day and you can find links to these in the resources section of the book.

Many depressed people seem to be outwardly coping in their lives. This is sometimes called 'smiling depression' – the person doesn't appear to be suffering, since they manage to present a happy public persona, but in private they are really struggling with their low feelings. They won't or can't admit to themselves what is happening, or else choose to hide it.

Very often it is those 'shoulds, oughts and musts' that are behind these performances of outward coping. At work we feel we should be able to cope with all that is thrown at us and we nod and smile in assent while secretly experiencing real difficulties. This is why it is important not to feel that depression or any other mental health issue is a stigma. It is important to allow yourself to recognize what is happening so that you can start dealing with the problem.

2. Thinking changes

These may include difficulty in making decisions, concentrating or remembering. A person may interpret things in an excessively negative way, see themselves as inadequate, unattractive or a bad person. They may be unhappy in their surroundings and see no prospects for their situation improving in future. Depressed people often attribute negative events to themselves, and so blame themselves for their situation, not the external situation or events that may be occurring. When people are depressed they often don't realize that their worldview has shifted in this way. People around them such as colleagues, friends and family may see the changes the sufferer themselves may not.

3. Physical changes

Having trouble getting to sleep or waking early can often be symptoms of depression. Changes in eating patterns resulting in weight loss or gain can also indicate a problem, as can changes in sex drive or simply a loss of interest in usual activities and pursuits. Aches and pains and excessive tiredness may also be warning signs. Some people also exhibit a heightened sensitivity to changes in their body and increased health anxiety – obsessing over bodily sensations and interpreting them as indications of serious illness.

4. Behaviour changes

Because of their decreasing interest and enjoyment of life, many people suffering from depression become noticeably less active. They may isolate themselves and start to feel it intolerable to join in with social activities. They start to have minimal communication with their partners and families, and avoid any activity that is not essential. Behavioural changes can include alterations in eating and drinking patterns, and starting or increasing the use of alcohol, tobacco or drugs. Sleeping routines may be altered and they may experience a loss of sex drive. They may get up late or spend long periods lying in bed or on the couch watching television.

Am I heading towards depression?

If you are concerned that you may be suffering from or heading towards depression then it might be a good idea to see how many of the following symptoms you have experienced over the last week:

- I have been feeling low

- I have been feeling tired and lacking in energy

- I have frequently felt irritable

- I have had trouble concentrating

- I have not been interested in the usual things I enjoy

- I have preferred to spend time on my own

- I have been feeling guilty

- I have been unable to see the point of anything

- I have been feeling useless

- I have thought of hurting myself

- I have felt very alone and isolated

- I have been troubled by aches and pains

- I have not felt able to cope when things go wrong

- I have felt despairing or hopeless

- I have been disturbed by unwanted thoughts or feelings

- I have difficulty getting to sleep or staying asleep

- I have been blaming myself for my problems

- I have done things to hurt myself

- I have thought about ending my life

- I have been unable to see any hope in future.

If you have been experiencing five or more of these symptoms for longer than two weeks it could well be that you are depressed or in danger of becoming depressed. It is important to check this out with your doctor. Make a list of exactly what you have been feeling and take it along with you – it is a lot easier if you have a checklist with you as it will help you be more specific and will aid the doctor's diagnosis. Take a friend too if you feel you may become too emotional to explain. Doctors are used to this, so don't feel embarrassed or ashamed.

REMEMBER THIS!!! A little knowledge can go a long way. You may understand what the symptoms of flu are and be on the lookout for them if you start feeling run down. You probably also have a good idea what to do to help yourself. But do you do the same with your mental health? Do you look out for the warning signs and look out for the difference between feeling a bit low for a couple of days and beginning to get ill with depression? Those negative thoughts that you carry round in your head are all having an impact on your internal body chemistry.

Of course, in any career there will be times when we need to work intensively for a short period of time. A pressing deadline, a new project, professional exams, moving premises or making presentations may require an extra burst of energy and dedication. You could find that you are experiencing some of the symptoms we have just discussed during this period. This is natural and to be expected – don't worry if you do find your sleep and eating patterns altered, or suffer waves of anxiety during the busy period. Often we can achieve more when we push ourselves to our limits over a short period. This will hopefully be followed by all the good feelings which come with the achievement of a goal. It is only if you are feeling low for continued periods when there is no obvious temporary change at work to blame that you should take such symptoms as a warning that you could be in a difficult place.

Admitting there is a problem

It is important to realize that depression is an illness like any other and you need to treat it as such. If you keep 'soldiering on' under very difficult circumstances, without giving yourself time to rest it is going to make it harder to get better. You may even need to consider taking some leave from work so you can give yourself a break. Having time out can help you to reflect and gain some perspective. You can't do that whilst you are in the middle of the situation that is having such an impact on you. I see many clients who have pushed themselves so far they have burnt out and run themselves into the ground.

A clinical depression episode lasts about six months on average. Receiving professional medical help such as a course of CBT therapy or medication can help reduce some of the symptoms, as well as lessen the damage that is done to professional and personal relationships. If your work situation is getting to you, taking some time out before the depression takes hold can help ward off the likelihood of sinking deeper: 'A stitch in time saves nine.'

Take feelings of depression seriously. Look after yourself and take a little time out before things escalate and force you to take a lot of time out. We will now look at some case studies to show how using CBT early on to manage your feelings can also help you get a handle on things before they escalate to the point that you need help from a trained professional.

Nadine

Nadine had just had her appraisal at work. Her boss was not happy with her performance; she was rated as underachieving. She had been struggling at work for a few months. Her workload had steadily been increasing and she felt overwhelmed. She regularly felt like crying on her way to work and recently she had cried in the toilets there. She had lost weight, she kept getting one cold after another and she felt sick most of the time. She didn't even enjoy weekends now, as the thought of going back to work on Monday loomed over her. She hadn't told anyone how she was feeling as she felt too embarrassed to admit what she saw as weakness and failure on her part. She started to slide into depression.

What do you think Nadine could have done to help herself with these negative thoughts and stop them from escalating. Try applying the Think Kit to her immediate upset. Remember, ABC:

Actual Situation
Belief
Consequence

What does she need to change in order to reduce the emotional upset to a more manageable level? By now you should be familiar enough with the Think Kit to identify the A, B and C yourself, and to come up with some suggestions of more helpful beliefs that Nadine could try to replace her unhelpful beliefs with. Then, having used techniques to rationalize the immediate upsetting feelings, she would be better able to think about how to improve her situation. Here are some suggestions of what Nadine could do:

- She could talk to a colleague about how she is struggling

- She could arrange another meeting with her manager to discuss how she could address the areas she was underperforming in

- She could request some training to help her

- She could ask if there was a mentor she could work with.

Let's get physical

Whilst CBT can help you with your mind, depression also responds well to using strategies which involve your body. We mentioned earlier that depression is very much affected by the levels of different hormones in your body, particularly serotonin, the 'happy hormone'.

Studies such as those by Professor Mark Mintun have found that people who are depressed have low levels of serotonin. Antidepressants, called selective serotonin reuptake inhibitors (SSRIs) work by preventing the body from reabsorbing its serotonin, thus maximizing the levels in your bloodstream.

It has also been found that aerobic exercise increases serotonin levels, thereby improving mood, so keeping as active as possible is an important way of staving off depression. On top of this, when you exercise hard, you release chemicals called endorphins into your body. Endorphins are the neurotransmitters produced in the brain that are responsible for relieving pain. They are another of the body's natural 'feel good' chemicals and also help to raise your mood.

Not many of us have jobs which involve a lot of exercise or time spent outdoors, but naturally it helps to keep mind and body healthy if you can incorporate exercise into your daily routine. If you have a desk job, there are some small things you can do to help yourself. Make sure you have a proper lunch break, and go outside and walk around for 30 minutes as part of it. Use the stairs instead of the lift. Find a local gym to visit after work before going home. The more you can do to stay active, even in small ways, the better you will feel.

It does take a lot effort to exercise when you are feeling low, but ironically that is exactly what you need to do in order to help boost your happy hormones. If you can incorporate at least three sessions of physical activity into your week, you will be making a great investment in yourself. Going outside in the day when you can also gives you a healthy boost, as we need sunlight for production of some vitamins, such as vitamin D. You can buy natural light boxes – place one on your desk for a couple of hours a day if you are finding it hard to spend time in the sunlight (especially difficult sometimes in winter).

Playing on physically interactive games consoles can be a substitute for joining a gym if the games get your heart-beat up sufficiently. They can also be very motivating as they log your personal fitness levels.

Find the activities that work best for you, just remember: keep active!

Plan your week

Recovery programmes for people who are coping with depression often include making a day-by-day plan. Having a plan helps to focus on the present and to experience a regular feeling of success as small goals are achieved. Breaking each day into manageable and realistic chunks helps you make your way along the road to recovery one step at a time.

Try introducing this kind of planning into your week. This does not have to mean making a comprehensive time-table of every single thing that you are going to do – you might just record a few key goals and milestones. There will always be changes and crises at work that will make your plans unrealistic some days, so don't be too hard on your-self if you fail to do everything that you set down.

If one does not know to which point one is sailing, no wind is favourable.

Seneca

Laughter, the best medicine

Laughter is another proven way of making yourself feel better and reducing stress. In the 1980s Dr Lee Berk's research showed that when we laugh, the levels of that infection fighter, immunoglobulin A, are raised. Even fake smiling raises them a little. Losing your sense of humour is something that happens under stress, and depressed people don't laugh a lot. Taking steps to bring some much-needed laughter back into your life can only be a good thing.

There is the well-known case of Robin Cousins, an American who in 1964 was suffering from a serious, debilitating illness called ankylosing spondylitis and was given only a few months to live. However, he believed in the power of positive thinking and laughter, and decided to check himself into a hotel room, hire a doctor to monitor him and watch Charlie Chaplin films endlessly. His condition went into remission. It is true that during this period he was also given injections of vitamins, but like Cousins himself I would like to attribute at least some of his recovery to the real power of laughter.

TRY IT NOW!

Make a list of films that make you laugh. Buy a couple of them on DVD and keep these at home. When life is getting too serious and you are feeling tired or a bit down, take out one of those films, sit back and laugh.

You can then increase your list to include other things that make you laugh, whether that is playing with a pet or reading a favourite column in a newspaper. Whatever works for you. Going out with colleagues from work for a fun group activity can also be a good idea, as it gives you the chance to mix on a different level and laugh together.

CASE STUDY

Arlo

Arlo was an engineer who worked in a very busy office. His job involved mostly carrying out site visits and writing up reports. His department became understaffed when vacant posts were not advertised in time and there was suddenly a lot of extra work to cover. Arlo helped his colleague out by covering some of her site visits for her, on top of his own. He felt quite exhausted but his colleague had been having problems at home and he wanted to help her out. Later in the month, Arlo had to take three days sick leave as he was ill with a virus. When he returned to work a lot of important tasks had piled up. He felt overwhelmed and panicky. He asked his colleague if she could help out by doing one of his visits for him. She made excuses, saying she was also busy. Arlo felt stung. He was upset that there was no reciprocal help for him. He continued to go in to work, dreading each day as he could not get on top of his workload. He couldn't shake off the cough he had been left with after his illness and he became increasingly tired and disillusioned.

This case study is a clear example of how what might seem like relatively minor stresses in a person's life can gradually build up until they have such a serious effect that the person starts sliding into depression.

What do you think?
What CBT steps could Arlo use?
What practical steps could he consider?

Although the CBT Think Kit is very useful when you feel ready to pay attention to your thinking, when you are feeling depressed it can be very hard to sort out the abstract issues of your thoughts and beliefs. So, for Arlo it may be helpful to offer some practical steps to go through first, before he thinks about tackling the root of the problem.

- The longer Arlo struggles on his own, the more likely it is that his persistent low moods will drop into a more chronic state of depression.

- Arlo needs to make an appointment with his doctor.

- He needs to tell a co-worker or his manager how he is feeling after the visit to the doctor.

- He may need to take some leave, or may even be signed off by his doctor to take some sick leave. This will give him a chance to rest so that he will be in a better position to start rationalizing his situation and to come up with a plan of action for work and home.

- When he starts feeling better, it might be good to introduce some regular activities into his daily life. It is well known that exercise is a mood lifter, and planning your days using a diary either on paper or on a device can help get your life under control and in perspective.

- When Arlo is less depressed he can start to address the attitudes and demands he places on himself regarding work, using the CBT Think Kit to work out which specific issues he is struggling with and working towards changing them.

To sum up

Depression is an illness, so treat it as you would any other. You are not superman or superwoman – everyone has limits on their ability to cope with life's daily struggles. If you find that you are feeling continuously low for no obvious reason it may unfortunately be that you are in danger of sliding into a period of depression. It is probably not worth dwelling on why this happens to some people and not to others – what matters is to recognize the symptoms and get some help.

The most important thing to remember is that no matter how bad it gets, if you take the right steps, black dog days can and will pass.

Matthew Johnstone

The key points

- Feeling low is natural, but it is important to know the symptoms of depression

- Recognize the warning signs of depression: changes in mood, thought and behaviour

- Keep active. Exercise releases endorphins into the body, which may help to cope with low moods

- Stick to a routine and find ways to make yourself laugh

- Follow practical steps to get to the root of the problem

---

7. CBT for low self-esteem at work

You yourself, as much as anybody in the entire universe, deserve your love and affection.

Buddha

Banish low self-esteem forever

To describe it as simply as possible, self-esteem is how you rate yourself. It is about how you value yourself and your behaviours, particularly when compared to others. This is a combination of the way you interpret what is going on around you and the self-talk that goes on in your head. With its varying demands and the ever-present need to achieve, the work place is a potential danger zone for developing worries and insecurities about yourself. These can include worries about:

- Your performance
- Your ability to manage others
- Your appearance
- Your professional status
- Whether people like you

This chapter will give you some simple techniques to help banish self-esteem problems and learn to like yourself.

Where does a sense of self come from?

Even as a child you start to build up a picture of the kind of person you are, based on the reactions of people at home and in other environments such as school. You get feedback like:

'Well done, you are a good girl.'
'Isn't Johnny clever, look what he has made.'

OR
'You are such a disappointment to us.'
'You will never amount to much.'

A piece of research looking at achievements of a minority group of school children in London in the 1980s concluded that the best thing a parent can give a child is a high sense of self-esteem. If you were brought up in an encouraging and supportive family, the chances are that it has really helped you to achieve your potential. Not everyone has that familial support, and even if they do, sometimes other elements of their life can be harsh and discouraging. All your life you are bombarded with unsolicited feedback. People will comment on your appearance, your personality, your performance at school and work. Your social life will be a myriad of constantly changing rules and norms. You may even be unfortunate enough to be bullied. All of these things can impact on your sense of self one way or another.

TRY IT NOW! Think back over the last week. Record any and all good feelings that you had on each day. Now, try to identify the situation or occurrence that triggered these feelings. Record the information in a table like this one:

	Good feelings	**Actual situation**
Monday		
Tuesday		
Wednesday		
Thursday		
Friday		
Saturday		
Sunday		

Look in detail at each of the good feelings and try to think about what it was specifically that you liked about yourself.

Now try the same exercise, but looking back over the week to spot any times you weren't feeling so good about yourself.

	Bad feelings	Actual situation
Monday		
Tuesday		
Wednesday		
Thursday		
Friday		
Saturday		
Sunday		

You may have found this second exercise easier! We are all very good at pointing out our own failings and dwelling on the things we don't like about ourselves. It's very easy to direct a great deal of negative thinking towards yourself.

When I have a client who is in this situation I get them to do an exercise which is called the 'sticky notes' experiment.

I ask the client to ask three people they know to tell them three things they like about them. They may feel quite embarrassed about doing this; often we are uncomfortable about hearing good things about ourselves. Getting through this discomfort is part of the exercise. If a client is not likely to see the people they have chosen to ask before the next session it is okay for them to phone or text. I then ask them to keep a record of the nine positive things they have been told.

In the next session I ask the client to read the nine things out to me. This is often quite an emotional thing to do. To hear positive things said to you from significant people in your life can be moving, insightful and even revelatory.

I write down each positive attribute they have collected on a separate sticky note. With their permission, I then stick the nine notes on their arm. I then ask them to re-tell me the issue that they were struggling with, related to considering themselves a 'bad person'. I write that on a sticky note as well, which I stick on the other arm.

I then ask them to take a look at their whole self covered in sticky notes. I ask the client to read out all the **positive** notes again. I then ask them to focus on the lone **negative** sticky note on their other arm. I then ask the client to consider a CBT question of the kind that we have met plenty of times in this book: how is focusing on that one mistake/misdeed/aspect of your appearance helping you? The answer is simple: it isn't.

If a client can be encouraged to look at their whole self, instead of one tiny aspect which is making them unhappy, then they will have to concede that they are full of positive attributes, skills, talents and qualities. There is already evidence of this with feedback from only three people. There are many more people that that in anybody's life. If they all gave one sticky note, think how the positive attributes would stack up!

 Try running through the sticky note experiment yourself. Without a third party such as a therapist to encourage you to ask others for these positive qualities you may feel a bit awkward, but persevere as you will probably be very surprised and pleased with the result. I have never known anybody come back and say they weren't taken seriously when they approached people for this exercise. We can get so busy and caught up in our lives we don't always have time to tell people how great they are. But, as a client once said to me: 'It's helpful to hear what your close friends think of you now rather than wait for your eulogy.'

 No one can take away those positive qualities you have. Don't put the whole of yourself down because of one mistake or one negative comment from someone else. Accept that you are basically a good person – sometimes you may mess up, because we all make mistakes, but it is *how you view* those mistakes that will determine their effect on your sense of self. We are all fallible human beings, not just you.

Of course in an ideal world everything you did would always work out well, you would always look great, you would have a fabulous job that paid extremely well and life would be without hassles. But we live in the real world and things are rarely, if ever, perfect. There are many challenges to our self-esteem, both in the workplace and in our personal lives. You have a choice – either allow these things to drag you down and make you think badly of yourself, or decide to accept yourself unconditionally.

So what if you're not always the front of the pack professionally? There is more to life anyway. As the Dalai Lama says: 'The planet does not need more "successful people". The planet desperately needs more peacemakers, healers, restorers, storytellers and lovers of all kinds.'

Look at me, look at me, look at me!

It is important for our survival that we are looked on positively by others when we are growing up. It is inbuilt that we rely on others for food, shelter, warmth and if we are lucky, love. So it is that a strong belief that almost all of us retain into adulthood is that we need the approval of others. For some people, usually because of particular issues they have with their upbringing or other past experiences, approval is something that they believe they need almost constantly.

If they don't receive constant feedback to confirm that they have it they can feel anxious and depressed. Their behaviour may come across as 'needy'.

Being needy is usually construed as a negative attribute. When someone is viewed in these terms they can be susceptible to bullying from others, which can be every bit of much of a problem in the workplace as in the schoolyard. When we fall prey to bullying behaviour it often means that on some level we are agreeing with the negative feedback that is being thrown at us. If you are able to accept yourself unconditionally in the way that we have been discussing, it can help you to stand firm in the knowledge that the negativity being directed at you is their problem, not yours.

Candy

Candy enjoyed her job as a nurse. She worked in the intensive care unit of a busy hospital and was very experienced. She worked shifts, often working nights.

Over the years Candy had gained weight, partly because her eating patterns were erratic due to the constant shift changes making it difficult to have a good routine for meals. She became increasingly unhappy with the way she looked and a cruel comment by some teenagers on the bus one day was enough to trigger a bout of real depression.

As part of her recovery, the doctor referred her to a CBT group treatment programme. There Candy learned to accept herself for the talented, skilled and kind person she was. She realized that one of her coping strategies for dealing with her stressful work place had been to eat. As a result she started to view herself differently. She could see that upsetting herself daily about her weight was not helping her. The programme helped her rationalize her thinking so that she had a healthy concern about her weight rather than an unhelpful fixation. Once she felt less upset she was able to look at ways to develop new constructive behaviours to tackle this concern. As a start she joined the 'Shape Up' group run by the same organization as the CBT group, which offered a well-structured holistic health programme.

Candy began to accept herself and not worry about what others thought. She had a badge made for herself which she proudly showed at the last session. It said: 'Your approval is not necessary'. The group gave Candy a cheer.

Although we might want to be approved of by everyone we meet, realistically, this is unlikely. If you can totally accept yourself, 'warts and all', and see that you are a fallible human being doing the best you can, then outside criticism and internal negative self doubts will not impact on you so much.

Being able to survive the negativity of others without being hurt by it does not mean that you should put up with it indefinitely. You may find there are some people who are negative and unpleasant towards you no matter how considerate and kind you are to them. You need to impose a limit on how many chances you will give another person in their behaviour towards you. Although you may want their approval, putting up with selfish, inconsiderate behaviour is not in your best interests. Some people advocate a 'three strikes and you're out' rule. That is, they give others three chances to reciprocate considerate behaviour and after the third, if the other person is still not coming up with the goods, they move on. CBT encourages you to make conscious choices about what is in your best interests in this way.

Gifts of happiness

The following case study illustrates an exercise called 'gifts of happiness'. As you will see it has quite a lot in common with the sticky note experiment except that it is carried out in a group. It can be a great workplace activity to bring a team together and increase everyone's self-esteem, particularly if you are in the middle of a difficult project or particularly busy period which has left people feeling run down.

Taki

Taki was a bike courier in the city. He wanted to study electrical engineering and he joined a local 'return to study' course to prepare him for taking a degree. It ran one night a week for twelve weeks and there were eleven other students on the course, from varied backgrounds. The group worked together very well and Taki got a lot from being able to talk to the other members. Many of them had insecurities about their ability to study and were lacking in confidence at the start of the course. The tutor encouraged them to voice their concerns and was very good at putting them at their ease. At the end of the course, the lecturer came in with some strips of paper. He asked each member of the group to write down one positive attribute about every other person on a strip of paper. Then he asked them to fold the pieces of paper over and place them in piles on the table next to each group member's name.

At the end of the evening, everyone was told to take home their own strips of paper and to sit down and open them when they had a quiet moment. The lecturer called them 'gifts of happiness'. When Taki saw the lecturer a year later he told him that receiving them had had a big impact on him. He said no one had ever given him that kind of positive feedback and encouragement before. He had not taken school seriously and not achieved much. He kept the gifts in a drawer and if he started to feel low or question himself, he would take them out and re-read them. They felt particularly valuable because they were from people who had shared experiences with him and had got to know him well.

In the end ...

... it is important to accept yourself. Although it is natural to want to be liked and to have other peoples' approval the fact is, this will not always happen. If you can develop your own perspective on the idea of self-esteem, one which is independent of the feelings of others, it will help you face challenges (both in the workplace and elsewhere) in a more consistent way. If you can accept yourself as being the best person you can be – even if you do sometimes make mistakes – you will find that your emotional barometer will be more stable. When you do mess up, and you will, after all, you are only human, then use the CBT Think Kit to rationalize what went on, accept it, learn from it and move on. Accept yourself fully and learn to smile at your personal foibles.

> *The worst loneliness is not to be comfortable with yourself.*
>
> Mark Twain

The key points

- Self-esteem is a dynamic concept; it can go up or down

- A sense of self can be affected by outside influences

- CBT can encourage you to go for a more stable model of self-acceptance

- It is not helpful to rate the whole of yourself based on one mistake or ill-advised action

- You are a person, not wholly good or bad, but an essentially worthwhile human being

- Collect the evidence of your skills, talents and many attributes

- No one can take them away from you. Don't allow a bully to cast doubt on yourself

- Don't rely on others to tell you who you are or who they want you to be

- You will never get everyone's approval. Don't dwell on it; be appropriately sad or disappointed but not upset

- Self-doubt is natural at times. Use the Think Kit to rationalize the concerns. Don't beat yourself up; be the best you can, for yourself

8. Maximizing your happiness at work

*The most beautiful fate, the most wonderful good
fortune that can happen to a human being, is to be paid
for doing that which he passionately loves to do.*

Abraham Maslow

Work and happiness – what do we expect?

As CBT points out, sometimes there are mismatches between what we expect and what we actually experience. A philosopher called Alain de Botton looks at the history of human survival – the move from small self-sustaining groups to the concept of employment. He writes that originally work was meant to be a drudge; something to be accepted and got on with. There was no expectation of enjoying it.

*We should temper our sadness at the end of our
holidays by remembering that work is often more
bearable when we don't expect it to reliably deliver
happiness.*

Alain de Botton

Nowadays, of course, things are rather different. Although a difficult economic climate means that a lot of us do feel lucky simply to have a job, we still often have other expectations of our work, which are tied to our feelings about how we want to live our lives in general. People talk a lot about 'job satisfaction'. This can mean different things to different people – perhaps for one person it means doing a job while they feel makes a positive difference in the world, which for another it might be doing a job which is always varied and challenging, or simply one which they feel pays them well for their skills.

Of course, most people want to get paid and as much as possible. We all want to have enough money to pay our bills, eat well and afford leisure activities. This is central to almost everybody's conception of a good life. How much importance you place on being able to afford luxuries such as holidays, electronic equipment, cars and expensive clothes will dictate just how important money is to you.

What might you expect from a job? Make a list of the things that you consider important. This might include things such as:

- To be paid fairly
- To do work you find interesting
- To work reasonable hours
- To have job security
- To be treated with respect
- To have a reasonable number of holidays

How many of these criteria do you feel your current job fulfils?

Unhappiness at work

Whatever your expectations may be, it is almost certain that your job does not meet all of them exactly as you would wish. It's all too easy to look around and find people who are 'doing better' than you in one way or another. Modern celebrity culture practically encourages this kind of envy and many of the people we see adorning the covers don't really seem to have earned their wealth and success through hard work. By contrast, people in essential vocational roles such as nurses, teachers and social workers are not always paid very highly, and this seems unfair.

CBT looks at this issue. The simple fact is: life is not fair. If we have expectations that it should be, and yet the evidence shows us that it isn't, we are setting ourselves up for a lifetime of unhappiness. Of course there are times when it is appropriate to feel indignant about something, and to take steps to change it, if possible. For example, we might discover that someone who is in the same role as us, who has been working with the company for less time, is actually getting paid more. In such a situation like that it is reasonable to feel some annoyance and to seek to do something about it. On the other hand, becoming upset and envious because someone you know, or even someone famous, has bought a car which you would really like is pointless – you cannot change the situation and focusing on it will only perpetuate your bad mood.

If you constantly focus on the negative aspects of your job, you will make yourself unhappy. If you find you are persistently dissatisfied with a lot of things then changing your job might be the answer, but that may not be possible right away. You need to accept that although your hours, working conditions or pay aren't ideal, for the moment they will have to do. If you are able to do this you will be in a better position to focus on the things in your life that still make you happy. You can use your energy more positively: to look for another job, upgrade your skills and training, and generally start being more proactive.

> *We make a living by what we get but we make a life by what we give.*
>
> Winston Churchill

Blocks to achieving happiness

It may be that you are in a job in which you could be perfectly happy, but that you have rigid beliefs which are preventing you from enjoying it as you should. These kind of blocks fall into three main categories, which are as follows:

Block type one

Thinking along the lines of:

> 'I must do well in all the tasks I do at work. My colleagues and bosses must approve of me.'

Block type two

Thinking along the lines of:

> 'Other people at work must treat me fairly and in the way that I want them to.'

Block type three

> 'I must work in an environment that suits me and in which I can get what I want.'

These three blocks could be classified as, **what I must do, what others must do** and **how the world should be.**

In a perfect world perhaps all three conditions would be met exactly as you would like. Perhaps there are some jobs where you would have the opportunities to use your talents, have the resources to achieve your best and have the support and encouragement of colleagues and management *all the time*. It sounds a bit too good to be true though, doesn't it? The reality is that even in a job that is close to perfect for you, sometimes things won't go exactly as you would like them to.

CBT would consider holding on to rigid beliefs like these irrational, because the simple fact of us having them does not mean that they will be met – at least some of the time they will not be. If we continue to hold these beliefs about ourselves, others and our work environment when the evidence shows that they are not the case, then we set ourselves up for disappointment and unhappiness. If, on the other hand, we can pinpoint what it is about the situation that is at odds with our beliefs, by using the CBT Think Kit, we can start reducing our unhappiness.

Release the blocks with CBT

Block type one – 'I must ...'

A common belief of this type is 'I must always do well.' With this, as with any 'I must...' belief the tendency is for negative feelings to snowball and for us to start making inferences about the kind of person that we must be if we fail to live up to the belief. Our thoughts quickly start to run along the lines of: 'I must do well and if I don't I won't be able to stand it. It's awful, and it will prove that I am a worthless person.' This way of thinking sets us up to feel anxious, depressed, self pitying and apathetic.

As usual we need to challenge this kind of automatic negative thinking. If you don't always do things perfectly, or if not every single one of your colleagues likes you, does that truly make you a worthless person? Would you judge someone else in the same situation so harshly? I doubt it.

Once you have identified and examined your beliefs in this way using the Think Kit, and found them to be inconsistent, you can start replacing them with new and more helpful preferences in the usual way – 'I would prefer to do well but if now and then a task doesn't work out perfectly then that's okay, and it doesn't mean I am a complete failure. Everybody makes mistakes.'

Block type two – 'Others must ...'

If we carry on insisting to ourselves that other people – such as colleagues – should behave in a particular way, when our experiences prove that they simply do not, we are setting ourselves up to feel angry, vindictive and resentful. This is the basis for office feuds, obstructive behaviour, bullying, ostracising of colleagues and a generally unhealthy working environment.

We can't change the behaviour of others. Other people can and will do whatever they want. You can, however, use the Think Kit to replace your unhelpful rigid beliefs with more helpful preferences. This does not mean you have to allow people to walk all over you – you can still behave assertively – but you can prevent yourself from being deeply affected when people behave in ways that disappoint you.

I once read that 'happiness is the best revenge'. Whilst I do not advocate revenge as a way of dealing with difficult people, happiness is a choice you can make for yourself, and choosing to be happy in spite of somebody else's behaviour removes any hold they might have had on you.

Remember that bullies get their satisfaction from knowing that they have had an impact on you.

 Smile in the face of adversity. It will do you good. It will raise those serotonin levels, take some of the tension out of the situation and help you focus on your happiness.

Block type three – 'The world must be …'

In exactly the same way as with our expectations of other people's behaviour, if we cling to rigid views about how the world should be – minimum disruption, maximum comfort – we are inevitably going to be disappointed when things don't work out that way.

We can choose to dwell on the negative aspects of our working world, such as:

1. Long hours
2. Tight deadlines
3. Malfunctioning equipment
4. No staffroom facilities
5. Antisocial shift patterns

But getting stuck in a spiral of negative thinking about these things is not going to change them. If you make that cognitive shift to a place of acceptance, where, in spite of not liking the situation, you won't be actively perpetuating negative feelings, you will maximize your happiness in a given situation.

Instead of thinking along the lines of: 'I hate that work is difficult and that I have to work such long hours. I can stand the office, it's unbearable. I may as well jump under a bus.' You can change your thinking to: 'Work isn't great, I would prefer not to have to work so hard in a job I don't like but I can stand it. It's not going to kill me. Spending all my time thinking about it is only sapping the enjoyment from other parts of my life, such as spending time with my friends.'

Happiness comes from the capacity to feel deeply, to enjoy simply, to think freely, to risk life, to be needed.

Thomas Jefferson

How to cheer yourself up at work

Traditionally, psychological research has focused on studying what things can 'go wrong' for a person, and how these can be fixed. However, in recent years a new branch of studies which focuses on enhancing happiness, strength of character and optimism has received a lot of attention. It is usually referred to as positive psychology. One psychologist, Marty Seligman has written much on the subject. Earlier in this book we looked at personality and its impact on the way we work. One particular trait, optimism/pessimism can be a particularly influential factor on our happiness.

One of Seligman's studies, conducted on a group of nuns in America, looked at the impact of optimism on lifespan. Seligman noticed one day when looking around the graveyard in a convent that some of the nuns were extremely long lived. He thought that as the diets, exercise regimens and general living conditions of all the nuns were similar he could investigate what other factors might account for some living such long lives. What he found was very surprising.

When they were young women and first joined the convent, each of the nuns had been asked to write a novitiate essay on the topic of why they wanted to be a nun. Seligman went to the libraries to study these essays and found that they fell into two main categories. Some nuns wrote about the joy and privilege they felt at being able to enter life in a convent, while others wrote more about obligations and duties. Seligman found that the nuns who had expressed joy and optimism upon entering the convent were the ones who went on to live the longest. The more dutiful group still lived for a long time, but did not attain the extraordinary longevity of the optimists. This seems impressive evidence of the real power of positive thinking.

How could this optimism affect me at work?

Living longer aside, being open and optimistic can have plenty of other positive effects. Studies have shown the following advantages to being optimistic:

1. Optimists report higher life satisfaction

2. Optimists have better overall health, suffering less from anxiety, depression and illness

3. Optimists have stronger immune systems

4. Optimists recover from surgery more quickly

5. Optimists demonstrate perseverance and higher resilience.

It is the last point on that list which is perhaps the most significant from a work perspective. Optimists don't tend to blame themselves when things go wrong. They look at the overall situation. When faced with adversity, they tend to look for ways they can act in order to improve things; they don't give in to the difficulties. It's not difficult to see how this attitude means that they will be more likely to achieve their professional and personal goals.

I should be so lucky

Research by Professor Richard Wiseman published in his book *The Luck Factor* has shown that people can increase their 'luck' in life. He conducted a large study and concluded that lucky people are not born that way, but that they are using four basic principles to create good fortune in their lives. Wiseman suggests that:

- Lucky people maximize and take advantage of chance opportunities

- Lucky people make good intuitive decisions and listen to their gut feelings

- Lucky people are optimistic about the future

- Lucky people do not dwell upon ill fortune; they take control of the situation and strive to overcome it

Professor Wiseman stresses that there is no mysterious metaphysical influence at work in any of these characteristics; it is simply the way that lucky people go about their life in the world that enhances their good fortune. They are always looking outward and are open to new experiences. When they experience negative events, they are proactive; they take steps to improve their situation.

If you think about it, it's common sense that an optimistic attitude will usually get you further in life. Imagine that a vacancy comes up in another department within a company for a role which sounds interesting and appealing. One employee, who is a pessimist, sees it and says 'What's the point of applying? I won't get it – they'll never shortlist me. I'll never get out of this department'

Another employee, who is an optimist, sees it and says 'I may as well apply for the job. If I don't apply then I definitely have no chance of getting the job. If I get an interview, it will be good experience even if they don't offer me the job. How will not applying help me? It won't. I will be disappointed if I don't get called but it won't be the end of the world.'

REMEMBER THIS!!! By now, I think you will have noticed how the CBT emphasis on the importance of the way we view events comes in. As Ralph Waldo Emerson said, 'Good luck is another name for tenacity of purpose'. You need to be proactive and maximize your chances of 'winning'. Start making your own luck.

We should also be prepared for the fact that success takes more than just being open-minded and thinking positively.

Those things will make sure that you spot opportunities when they come your way, but after that there is another key ingredient to any good career: hard work. Reading biographies of successful people often reveals that they have overcome adversity in one form or another.

An inspiring figure to consider here is the actor Michael J Fox, who was diagnosed with Parkinson's disease (which usually affects elderly people) when he was just 30 years old. Parkinson's is a degenerative neurological condition, the most obvious symptom of which is the way that it can make the sufferer shake or tremble. Michael J Fox struggled secretly with the disease for seven years before revealing his condition to the public. He initially refused to accept the diagnosis and went into denial about it. It was only after a chaotic, alcohol-fuelled period of his life which nearly cost him his marriage and family that he went to another doctor who confirmed the diagnosis. Since that time he has continued to build a highly successful acting career and is also an outspoken campaigner for research into a cure for Parkinson's disease. He could have simply allowed the distress of having to cope with this illness to stifle his career but in the end he actively strove to overcome it, and has reaped the rewards.

Talent alone will not guarantee success; it takes a great deal of effort, time and persistence to succeed, and Michael J Fox is an inspirational example of this.

Life is great. Sometimes, though, you just have to put up with a little more crap.

Michael J Fox

The more you get involved with things, actively seeking out experiences and maximizing your effort, the more likely you are to be 'lucky'. Out of twenty jobs you may apply for, you may only get one interview – but if you apply for only one job then you greatly reduce your chances of getting an interview at all.

Gill (the author)

When I was a guest lecturer on cruise ships people often used to come up to me and say how lucky I was to have such a great job. However, I would never have ended up doing it at all had I not started approaching life differently. I am not a natural optimist – my frequent whining child and teen-ager about the unfairness of life attested to that, as did the anger with which I used to react when I didn't get a job I had applied for.

Later in life, however, I started training in CBT therapy. Learning about CBT helped me to rationalize my thinking and to stop blaming the world and other people when things didn't go my way. I started to be more proactive and open to new experiences.

One summer, I decided to sign up for a week-long cookery course for people wanting to work as cooks in ski chalets. I had always loved cookery at school but had chosen to continue with Latin instead when given the option. I was 50 and at the time I had no intention of working in a ski chalet – I just thought it would be a more interesting holiday than sitting on a beach for a week. As it turned out, I loved the course; it was exhausting but I was very happy and found it was an environment I felt at home in.

The next year, after a bereavement, I decided to take a 'gap year'. The opportunity to work in a ski chalet came up, advertised on a website called 'adventure jobs' which I had subscribed to on a whim. I went to work at a chalet in France for a few months. I enjoyed myself, and so I kept visiting the website periodically. One day I saw a job advertised by Oxford University, working on board the *Queen Mary 2*, managing the guest lecture programmes on transatlantic crossings.

In my new spirit of 'nothing ventured, nothing gained' I applied. I thought it highly unlikely I would be considered because of my age but nevertheless I updated my CV and emailed my application. After a couple of rounds of interviews, to my surprise and delight I got the job. My boss told me later that the most significant aspect of my CV was the chalet maid experience. That job required customer service skills, patience, resilience, enthusiasm and a willingness to work long hours. My academic qualifications were relevant too, but the experience of working in the leisure industry gave my CV the edge.

On top of all my other work, I was asked to write a series of lectures for the spa on board the ship but a lack of time meant that I was unable to deliver them. However, an art lecturer who I mentioned this to by chance suggested that I send my lecture titles to his agent. This brought about three bookings to lecture on cruise ships the following year. Looking back at the chain of events that led me there, I think it is pretty clear that if I had not changed my attitude to life and started being more inquisitive, optimistic and proactive, I would never have got the job.

Luck is a matter of preparation meeting opportunity.
Oprah Winfrey

Are you an optimist or a pessimist?

Do you know if you are naturally an optimist or a pessimist? One general way of checking out your attitudes to life is to complete a simple life satisfaction questionnaire.

On a scale of 1–7, how would you rate:

Your life in general
Your family life
Your personal life
Your financial situation
Your health
Your career

Add up the scores for each answer.

6–26 – a low score, indicating a relatively low level of life satisfaction

27–32 – a medium score, indicating a reasonable level of life satisfaction

33–42 – a high score, indicating a high level of life satisfaction

---

Generally an optimistic person will be more satisfied with their life, and so will score more highly on this test than a pessimistic person. Your results should give you some indication of your general outlook on life. It can also help you to identify which specific areas you may want to work on to improve your overall life satisfaction. You can identify specific feelings of discontent, examining your beliefs in these areas and working towards changing them. Once you have done that, you will naturally start behaving in a more positive, proactive way and you will soon begin to reap all kinds of benefits as a result.

You will spend a good deal of your waking life at work so ideally you should spend as little time as possible feeling unsettled and discontent whilst you are there. There will probably be times when you take a job out of financial necessity. That is life. If you can use CBT to rationalize the more tedious or challenging aspects, it can help you to change the way you view your job, so you aren't continually feeling angry, depressed or anxious. Use these strategies to release the blocks to your feeling content at work. Of course, there are times when work can seem to be taking over your life and getting in the way of you making the changes that you want to make. Finding an appropriate balance between work and the rest of your life is something that we will look at in the next chapter.

The key points

- Knowing what we hope to gain from work can be a helpful exercise

- Pinpointing areas of work that do not meet our expectations can be a useful starting place for identifying the origins of our dissatisfaction

- Dwelling on the negative aspects of your job can perpetuate thinking loops which cause discontent

- The Think Kit can be applied to help you reduce discontent and identify constructive ways of coping

- Devising a personal action plan for future goals is a positive way forward

- If you are naturally a more pessimistic thinker, you will have to work harder to change your negative views about work

- There are strategies you can employ to enhance you happiness at work

- Learning about how other people have coped with adversities in their careers can be motivating

- Be pro-active, get out there and increase your chances of changing your life

---

9. Balancing work and life

One of the symptoms of approaching a nervous breakdown is the belief that one's work is terribly important

Bertrand Russell

Working hard at a job you enjoy can feel great. If, even during the busiest times, you are still feeling the buzz – tired but happy – then you probably have the right balance between work and the rest of your life. But if you are so constantly tied up with the demands of your job that you feel that it pretty much *is* your life, then it is likely that you have the balance wrong. There is probably only so long you will be able to carry on if this is the case – you could be heading for a burnout.

There are various problems which people encounter in their working lives today, including:

- Working days not having a clearly defined beginning and end

- The boundaries between work life and home life becoming blurred

- Technology meaning that we can be accessible at any time and in any place

- 'Workaholism' – addiction-like dependence on work

- Putting in very long hours in the workplace late at night or early in the morning

- Inner conflict between our personal desires and what our job requires us to do

- Prioritizing work over personal plans

- Fatigue from over-work

- Work stress affecting interpersonal and sexual relationships.

The Work Foundation states that work–life balance is 'about people having a measure of control over when, where, and how they work. It is achieved when an individual's right to a fulfilled life inside and outside paid work is accepted and respected as the norm, to the mutual benefit of the individual, business and society.'

We have seen that pressures and anxieties can give rise to psychological distress and often physical symptoms of discomfort. The pressures people come under, frequently as a result of discovering once in the job that the demands are greater than anticipated, can have a deleterious effect on their health and well-being. People sometimes put themselves under even greater pressures because of their beliefs about the job and the responsibilities that it entails – they may feel they need to stay in touch with work constantly, work at home in the evenings and weekends, and prioritize work over their personal life. The insecurities in global markets and the effects this has had on employment opportunities in the 21st century are well known. As a result many people feel insecure in their job (if they are lucky enough to have one) and feel that they must work extra hard to ensure that they keep it.

The term 'workaholic' seems to have become part of our vocabulary around the 1970s to describe a person addicted to work or who, for some reason, works a great deal. It could refer to a person who loves their work and therefore wants to be doing it all the time, or it could refer to someone who feels compelled to put in long hours out of a sense of duty or necessity. It is not necessarily a negative term but the consequences of the balance of someone's life being heavily weighted towards work could be that other areas of their life are neglected or in fact nonexistent because of a lack of time.

Are you a workaholic?

Here is a simple questionnaire to encourage you to take stock of your working patterns:

Do you respond to non-urgent calls, texts and emails which are work-related in the evenings and at weekends?

Do you voluntarily work long hours?

Do you find it difficult to delegate?

Do you find it difficult to say 'no' to work requests?

Do you find it difficult to relax and 'switch off'?

Do you have problems getting enough sleep?

Do your family, friends or partner (if you have one) complain they don't see enough of you?

Is your self-esteem based largely on your work?

If you have answered 'yes' to one or two of those questions, it could simply be that you are dedicated to your work, which is not a problem. It is important for you to be on your guard, though, as the line between dedication and obsessive devotion is a fine one.

If you answered 'yes' to more than two questions, this could indicate that your work patterns are heading towards problematic workaholism. You may want to consider the possibility that this could be affecting your health and relationships, and in the long term possibly your career.

The point is that you need to keep an eye on how your working patterns are evolving and be aware if they start to have detrimental effects on the rest of your life. A short burst of long hours and weekend working may be what is needed for a special project but if you work like that constantly something or someone will eventually start complaining.

If you are a person who loves their work and are happy to devote most of your waking life to it then that is your choice. You probably get a lot of pleasure from being so involved in your work. It may be a problem for others around you, but you will need to weigh up when prioritizing work is compromising your social life and relationships and make decisions about this.

If, on the other hand, you are a person who feels pressured into working excessively in their job not by choice but because of deadlines, workloads, and relentless demands, with a result that you don't have enough time for yourself or other significant people in your life, then this is problematic. It will almost certainly result in a build-up of internal tensions which may express themselves as feelings of stress, anxiety, depression and anger of the kinds we have already examined earlier in the book.

It is important to take time out to assess what is happening for you if you are so involved with work. Some people find that by the time they stop to take stock, perhaps forced to do so by a crisis, significant people in their life have stopped looking for or expecting support and have organized their lives without them. The common signs of emotional distress are listed on page 27 – be on the lookout for them. Don't wait until a crisis forces you to take a look at what has been happening in your life.

Coping behaviours

When your life is very heavily weighted towards work you may start engaging in coping behaviours that, in the long term, could be detrimental to your health. We may turn to activities which help relieve tensions immediately and temporarily. Things like buying chocolate at the petrol station on the way home, the odd glass or two of wine to relax when you finally get in, a takeaway meal as a treat when you have no food readily available in the house. Other activities could include smoking or the use of recreational drugs, online gambling or repeated visits to other sites such as Facebook.

The occasional inclusion of a pleasurable 'prop' may help you to get by now and then. This in itself is not a terrible thing; we can't be expected to be complete stoics, denying ourselves of the odd glass of wine if we fancy, but we need to keep things in perspective. My dad had a strong work ethic and a naturally CBT-like attitude to life. One of his stock phrases was: 'Everything in moderation.'

What can happen when we are under prolonged stress is that these occasional diversions can become a regular habit. We may start to indulge in our coping strategy of choice more frequently. These new habits can become addictive. You need more to give you that same feeling of relief and you need it more often. Food addictions may mean that you increase in weight to unhealthy levels and addictions to other substances can seriously affect your health in other ways.

It is very hard to manage addictions but CBT treatments have been found to be both helpful and effective. In the first instance you can try to get burgeoning habits under control yourself by applying the CBT Think Kit. Shaking ingrained behaviours of this kind can be extremely difficult

– it's almost as if, for every time the habit gave you temporary relief, you have to go through an equal amount of discomfort now to break it. You have to forego short term pleasure for long term gain. You have to go through these discomfort zones to progress. Having trained support for habits which have really taken hold is advisable so don't hesitate to see your doctor or another health professional if you find you are unable to make progress on your own. It is hard for family and friends to provide this support with these kinds of problems as it puts extra responsibility onto both them and you. An independent professional is not going to be personally affected by your problems, they are trained not to be.

The people around us

Human beings have not evolved to live solitary existences. Apart from anything else, it is more efficient to live in social groups and to perform different roles within that group.

We evolved to live in cooperative societies, and for most of human history we depended on those groups for our lives. Our need for social acceptance emerged as a mechanism for survival, which is why having the support of those around still feels incredibly important to us, in spite of the fact it is rarely a matter of life or death nowadays. In difficult times it is important that we feel able to turn to the people close to us to ask for help – we may be able to help ourselves with the CBT Think Kit, but any burden is lessened by sharing it.

In today's busy society, it is comparatively rare for an extended family to all live geographically close to each other; the original natural sources of support are being replaced with different social structures. Many of us live long distances from our parents and families and often in different countries. The common sources of support in modern societies include:

- Friends

- Work colleagues

- Partners and spouses

- Interest group members

- Healthcare staff, doctors, practice nurses, community health teams

- Social networks

- Helplines

 THINK ABOUT IT Make a list of three people in your life you would turn to if you needed some help.

You may find it hard to think of three people that you would be able to go to about absolutely any problem. It can be hard to tell family or friends when you are struggling. Often people hide their struggles, either not wanting to burden others, or else because they feel ashamed of needing help. But as we have seen, the longer you keep anxieties and concerns to yourself the more likely things are to escalate.

Imagine a friend of yours has stopped meeting up with you and doesn't return your calls. You don't like to persist in ringing because you don't want to pry. However, you subsequently discover that his wife left him three weeks ago and since then he has been trying to both care for the children and go to work.

How would you have felt if this friend had rung and explained why he had been out of communication? Would you have been angry if he told you of his difficulties? It is much more likely that you would have wanted to see if you could help your friend in some way.

The point is, if we don't ask for help when we need it how are people to know? It is unlikely we would judge others as weak or abandon them in their time of need, so why would we assume that they would treat us that way?

Being proactive

But while the support of people around you can help to see you through difficult times, unless you take steps to live the kind of life that you want to, then problems will keep rearing their heads again and again. You need to be prepared to make an effort – to analyze the ways in which you could be happier and take steps to make improvements.

Scott

Scott was lonely and felt isolated by his lack of social life. He worked very hard and frequently was the last to leave the office and took work home at the weekends. When he wasn't work-ing, he was playing computer games. At the weekend, he went shopping for the basics and occasionally visited the cinema on his own. He didn't meet up with anyone. Whilst in themselves these behaviours and chosen lifestyle are not a problem, Scott was feeling anxious and depressed about the fact he was not sharing his life with a partner and did not have many friends. As a result he went to his GP for help and was referred to a CBT therapist.

It's easy to spot the rigid belief that caused Scott problems: as long as the evidence showed that he didn't have strong ties to someone special in his life and didn't have many friends, and as long as he clung on to the belief that he 'must have someone', he made himself anxious and some-what depressed.

His irrational thinking started chaining into 'I must be unattractive. No one likes me. I have no social skills. I am destined to always live on my own, never have a family and become a lonely recluse.' He was catastrophizing about himself, others and the world. This led to him continuing with unhelpful patterns of behaviour – he stayed in and didn't mix with others. This seemed to confirm the validity of his beliefs.

His therapist pointed out to him that as long as he held these beliefs and continued to think like this, he would continue to feel anxious and depressed, continue to spend his time on solitary activities and so remain on his own. He was exhibiting self-defeating behaviour. He needed to adjust his beliefs to something along the lines of 'I would prefer to have someone in my life and it is sad that I haven't but that doesn't make me an unlovable person. As long as I continue to shut myself away, I will continue to be on my own.'

CBT therapists often set homework for clients to carry out in between sessions. In order to help Scott change the way he viewed his situation and to help him reinforce more positive patterns of thinking he needed to involve himself in some new activities. The therapist asked Scott to iden-tify three places or activities which he felt would bring him into contact with other people with similar interests to his own. He liked going to the cinema, he loved cooking and was interested in vintage cars. Scott and the therapist then agreed his homework; he would ask at work and post an invitation on Facebook to see if anyone wanted to go to the cinema to see a film with him that week. He would sign up to attend Indian cooking classes, and he would research a local vintage car club with a view to joining it.

The therapist questioned Scott on what obstacles might make completing the homework difficult for him. This is an important stage when preparing to make life changes; the therapist challenges the client before the event, so that they are better prepared to deal with these obstacles if they do actually appear. You can think through potential obstacles on your own, too.

Scott said that he was nervous about posting the invitation on Facebook, as he might be seen as 'a loser'. His therapist pointed out that going through discomfort zones like this is essential to bring about change and move forward. They discussed what the worst thing that could happen was and together rationalized that even if no one posted back about the cinema proposal it was highly unlikely that people would think he was a loser for suggesting it – he would not react that way if someone else did the same thing. If nobody wanted to come, Scott could stand it; he wouldn't like it, he would be disappointed but it wouldn't be such a big deal – he could try again in a couple of weeks. He wouldn't upset himself by interpreting the lack of response as confirmation that he was an unlikeable, unlovable person. Perhaps people were just busy. By being proactive he was increasing his chances of company, whether or not he got the response he wanted initially.

If Scott had continued to stay at home bemoaning the fact he had no friends, this would certainly have remained the case. But within a month Scott had been to the cinema twice with friends, started his cookery classes, and was looking forward to the vintage car group's weekend rally. After a couple of months, his confidence growing, he also started up a 'come dine with me' group at work, which proved very popular.

Scott had changed his thinking and so his behaviour, the two positively reinforcing each other as he made progress. He took risks, being proactive in choosing new ways of behaving. He did feel anxious on many occasions when he was engaging in these new behaviours he had picked for himself, but by using the CBT Think Kit to rationalize his worries, he saw things through. It takes hard work and lots of practice to do this; no one can do it for you. However, the more opportunities you create for yourself the more chance there is of things turning out the way you want them to.

- Do I feel my life is in balance with my work?

- What aspects of my work–life balance would I like to change?

- What is stopping me making these changes?

- How would I like my work–life balance to be?

- My perfect job – what would my perfect job be in terms of work–life balance?

- Make a list of three things you would like to change

- Look at the first one – make two lists, one of what is stopping you from doing this and the other 'What I would need to start to do'

It is worth doing a self-check like this regularly to make sure that life is not controlling you, as opposed to the other way round. You have a responsibility to look after yourself – I often say to clients that the only person who is really responsible for your happiness is you. Other people can make your life easier, add to your happiness and enhance your sense of well-being by their actions towards you, but basically it is down to you. There is a book called *How to be Your Own Best Friend* by Paul Hauck, a CBT psychologist, that I like to give to clients to read if they have trouble looking out for themselves. It emphasizes that putting your own well-being first is not necessarily selfish in a negative sense. It talks about the Buddhist concept of 'enlightened self interest' as a healthy way of being. It is about making conscious choices, not feeling guilty if you have to say 'no' sometimes. In the next chapter we will look at other helpful practices that can maintain or increase your sense of well-being and happiness.

The key points

- Working conditions are constantly changing

- Pressure from demands at work may often seem to spiral out of control

- A certain amount of pressure at key times can be motivating; however, continual demands that seem to outweigh your ability to meet them can be detrimental to your well being

- We may engage in coping behaviours that we start to rely on and become addicted to

- Be aware of changes in your habits or feedback from others showing concern for the changes in your behaviour

- Use the Think Kit to help you pinpoint any distress you find you are experiencing

- Get extra help if your unhealthy coping strategies have taken a firm hold

---

10. And ... relax

Tension is how you think you should be. Relaxation is who you are.

Chinese proverb

In addition to confronting problems and overcoming obstacles, it is important to include time in your life to simply relax. Nowadays we seem to live in a reactive way – constantly responding to the demands of work, domestic chores, family and friends. Putting some structured relaxation time into your day can help to prevent problems from spiralling out of control by giving you the mental space you need to analyze things and apply the CBT Think Kit. In this chapter we will look briefly at a few very simple relaxation exercises – consider incorporating one of them into your daily routine.

 Here is a very simple relaxation exercise which you can quickly do whenever you have a spare moment. It might be particularly useful to find a quiet spot to do it if you are having a particularly fraught day at work.

- Put down your book or e-reader.

- Sit up in a relaxed but straight-backed posture.

- Imagine a wave of relaxation flowing from the top of your head slowly all the way through your body down to your toes.

- Look straight ahead and take in your immediate surroundings.

- Now look beyond them. Gently turn your head to scan a wider area.

- Take three deep breaths, in … and out.

There, you've started to widen your view, consciously relax and take some 'time out'.

Another helpful action that you might want to tack on to the end of this exercise is to shrug your shoulders up and down to release tension. Taking each arm around in wide circular 'windmills' can also really help to loosen up your body, particularly after time spent hunched over a computer.

Obviously how often you are able to do this exercise (or any other relaxation technique) may depend on your location. Wildly waving your arms around might seem a little strange to others in your office, though perhaps you could incorporate a 'break out' exercise time for you and your colleagues into the working day. I once gave presentations to a new and dynamic finance company who were working in a converted 19th-century factory. There were plenty of open spaces, sitting areas, places to get food and drink and even a couple of pool tables. The employees were encouraged to 'break out' when they needed to take time away from their screens. The productivity figures for this building showed an increase compared to other branches of the organization based in more conventional office spaces around the country. Proof, if any were needed, that relaxation isn't just 'slacking off'.

> *No matter how much pressure you feel at work, if you could find ways to relax for at least five minutes every hour, you'd be more productive.*
>
> Dr Joyce Brothers

We've already discussed how important it is to be able to stop thinking about our work at the end of the day, but for many of us this is easier said than done. However, there are relaxation exercises geared towards helping us to 'switch off' like this. Here is one you can try after a stressful day at work.

 Find a quiet place to do this where you will not be disturbed. Prepare for a ten minute time-out session for yourself. Switch off any electronic gadgets and make yourself comfortable – either sitting in a chair or lying on a bed.

- Close your eyes. Pinpoint in your mind what it is that has wound you up or upset you that day.

- Say to yourself, either out loud or in your head 'I am not going to upset myself, I am going to relax into calm.'

- Smile to yourself.

- Breathe in, counting to three in your head and feeling the air flowing into your body. Become aware of a warm, heavy feeling suffusing your body, spreading out through your limbs.

- Breathe out, counting to three. Focus on the breath leaving your body. Feel the your body relaxing as it goes.

- Repeat this as many times as you need to, breathing in and out, until you feel calm and the worries of your working day have been left behind.

- Rest.

You will notice that a feature of both of the exercises we have looked at so far is deep, measured breathing. The very essence of our being is our ability to breathe. Without breath there is no life. Breathing correctly is very important, as our breath can have an impact on our emotional state.

When we get agitated or upset our breathing is affected. We may breathe faster, or take more shallow breaths. This can affect how much oxygen we are getting into our bodies, and oxygen is of course essential for the body and mind. Shallow, rapid breathing can then produce other symptoms that can in themselves be anxiety provoking. Dizziness, lightheadedness, tightness in the chest, ringing in the ears and even visual disturbances can occur when the oxygen levels in a person's bloodstream fall.

It's hardly surprising, then, that a lot of relaxation techniques involve concentrating on the breath. Getting into new habits of deeper breathing will help your body to function as it should, and help you to remain calm and in control.

THINK ABOUT IT

How are you breathing right now?

Hold one hand on your chest and the other on your abdomen. As you breathe in and out, the hand on your chest should be almost stationary. The hand on your abdomen should move outward as you breathe in and inward as you breathe out. Your breaths should be even and regular.

If you find that you are not breathing correctly, regularly practising the relaxation exercises we have looked at can certainly help. Sometimes, however, it is useful to have professional supervision when trying to retrain your breathing. Meditation classes can offer you this support, and of course are an excellent way of booking some relaxation time into a busy schedule.

Mindfulness meditation

Meditation has been practised in some countries for thousands of years. Actual meditation practices vary from sitting quietly contemplating a candle's flame to visualization exercises, but all meditative techniques share the aim of calming the mind and slowing its racing thoughts. Breathing is very important in almost all meditative practices.

In the 20th century a form of meditation called mindfulness has developed, which particularly encourages its practitioners to be aware of the present moment and to focus on the now. Doing so gives you respite from problems, negative thinking, and other daily hassles.

Mindfulness meditation has been found to be a useful tool in treating depression, anxiety disorders and obsessive compulsive disorder. It is a form of therapy now recommended by the National Health Service in the UK. One of the originators of mindfulness was Jon Kabat-Zinn, from Massachusetts University, who also discovered that practising mindfulness helped patients with chronic pain to cope with their discomfort.

The body scan

The following is a relaxation exercise commonly used in mindfulness practice to give you a little taster. It is called the 'body scan'. If you have limited time in which to carry out the exercise you may want to set the alarm on your phone (in gentle tones) to bring you back into alertness after about 10 minutes, otherwise you may lose track of time. If you do the exercise last thing at night when you are in bed, you can just allow yourself to drift off to sleep when you are finished.

- Lie down or sit comfortably in a chair somewhere quiet.

- Close your eyes and focus on your breathing. Breath in ... and out. Make sure that your breaths are deep and regular.

- Now slowly turn your attention to your body, starting with your feet. Become aware of the sensations in them. Don't make any judgement about these sensations, simply acknowledge them to yourself.

- When you are ready, move on to your legs. What do they feel like? Move up through your calves, knees and thighs and feel the weight of them pressing down. Become aware of the sensations in them, acknowledge them and, when you are ready, move on.

- Focus on your hips and groin and go through the same process.

- Move on up your body, visualizing each area in turn and allowing yourself to feel the sensations in each, finishing with your head.

- Now allow your whole body to feel heavy and completely relaxed. Stay like this for as long as you like.

If you would like to learn more about mindfulness there are plenty of resources to help you. A good starting point would be *Introducing Mindfulness*, another book in the Practical Guides series. Remember, building some structured relaxation time in to your daily routine can help to give you the space and calm you need to rationalize your problems and tackle issues using the CBT Think Kit.

The end of the book, the start of your new thinking?

My aim in this book has been to share some of the helpful practices which I have learned over the last twenty years working in CBT therapy. If you can take something away from this book that helps reduce anxious feelings, raise depressed spirits or enhance your everyday wellbeing, then it will have been worth writing. I have referred to various books and resources along the way. There is a list of these at the end of the book to help you take things further.

We all experience tough times and have discomfort zones to go through and when things aren't going well in your work it can affect your whole life. The more proactive you are about tackling difficulties and the more you examine your thinking and behaviour, the more you will find things improving for you. As Aristotle said, 'The unexamined life is not worth living.'

Sometimes you will have to dig deep to find the inner resources to overcome obstacles, sometimes you will need to call on others to help you, but it will be worth it. You *can* think your way to a happier, more balanced life.

I am not going to wish you luck – you know by now you can change your own luck. Believe in yourself. You are a unique person with many skills, talents and special qualities that no one can take away from you. Keep a sense of humour, have fun and start making the life you want.

Life is not a dress rehearsal

Rose Tremain

 The key points

- Plan for relaxation
- Make a conscious decision to switch off from work
- Short periods of relaxation can make you more productive
- Plug in your own charger and replenish your power source
- Being aware of your breathing patterns can help you relax
- Mindfulness meditation encourages you to be fully present in the 'now' of everyday life
- Get into the habit of practising relaxation exercises

Different types of therapies

I have often found that people can get confused with all the different types of doctors, therapists, types of therapy, and need some more information about how to go about finding the best help for themselves. Human beings are individuals. There is no 'one therapy fixes all', and it is important that you feel comfortable with the therapist. Treatments will vary according to the medical and theoretical background they derive from.

The resources section at the back of this book lists numerous links to professional organizations, many of which list their accredited therapists.

Below are some different types of therapies.

Psychiatrist – a medically qualified doctor who has had further training and qualifications in specialising in mental health and wellbeing

Psychologist – has a degree in psychology, often further degrees and specialisation in a particular branch of psychology – eg:

    Counselling psychology
    Sports psychology
    Child psychology
    Cognitive therapy
    Behaviour therapy

CBT therapy
Person Centred Counsellor
Psychosynthesis Counsellor
Gestalt therapists
Acceptance and Commitment Therapy
Eye Movement Desensitisation Therapist (E.M.D.R.)
Neuro-Linguistic programming therapy
Hypnotherapy
Mindfulness Based Cognitive Therapy (M.B.C.T.)
Positive Psychology.

Resources

Organizations offering advice and therapy

www.mind.org.uk
MIND is a UK-based organisation that publishes on many topics relating to mental health.

www.babcp.org.uk
The British Association for Behavioural and Cognitive Therapies provides information on CBT and how and where to find a therapist.

www.sane.org.uk
A mental health awareness organisation providing information and support.

www.undoingdepression.com
For information and help on depression.

www.samaritans.org.uk
Available 24 hours for support for distress, despair or suicidal thoughts.

www.anxietyuk.org.uk
A specialist organisation for anxiety issues.

www.ocduk.org
For specialist information regarding Obsessive Compulsive Disorders.

www.netdoctor.co.uk
For medical information on all aspects of patients' ailments.

www.getselfhelp.co.uk
Practical guides on CBT and self-help; and resources, information and worksheets.

www.fearfighter.com
An online CBT package accessed through the NHS services.

www.bemindful.co.uk
A mental health foundation including a directory of courses.

www.mbct.co.uk
The official UK website for Mindfulness-based Cognitive Therapy.

www.actionforhappiness.org
A movement to create positive change, with useful resources and video clips.

www.positivepsychology.org
The University of Pennsylvania's Positive Psychology
Centre Director's website – Martin Seligman. Many useful
resources, tests and questionnaires.

www.workmad.co.uk
For information and links to other sites and practical
information for professional and personal use.

www.centreforconfidence.co.uk
For information and research on positive psychology,
optimism, happiness, resilience and a blog link to current
affairs.

www.bangor.ac.uk/mindfulness
Provides courses and training in mindfulness and
resources.

http://www.bbc.co.uk/science/humanbody/mind/
surveys/personality/index.shtml
Self-test your personality.

http://www.bbc.co.uk/health/emotional_health/
mental_health
For information and advice on a wide range of mental
health issues including anxiety and depression.

**www.depression-anxiety-stress-test.org/
useful-links-and-information**
For useful information and links for stress and depression.

www.centreforconfidence.co.uk
For information about psychology subjects such as
happiness, optimism, resilience and attitudes.

www.ippanetwork.org
The International Positive Psychology Association, with
members that include researchers, students and the
general public.

www.bemindfulonline.com
A four-week online course run by the Mental Health
Foundation.

www.mbct.com
For CDs and tapes recorded by Jon Kabat-Zinn.

www.gaiahouse.co.uk
For information on Insight meditation retreats in the
Buddhist tradition in the UK.

www.internationaljournalofwellbeing.org
Open access to its academic journal sponsored by the
Open Polytechnic of New Zealand.

www.bda.uk.com www.nutrition.org.uk and
www.eatwell.gov.uk
For information on nutrition, well-being and health.

www.spiceuk.com
An adventure, sports and social group.

http://www.ecehh.org/publication/does-living-coast-improve-health-and-wellbeing
The Blue Gym project for mental health and well being.

http://www.cuc.ac.uk/research/cuc-research-programme
The University of Exeter Green Gym project.

http://www.sensationalcolor.com/color-messages-meanings/color-meaning-symbolism-psychology
Kate Smith and the colour green.

www.adventurejobs.co.uk
For regular updates on many kinds of work opportunities.

www.natives.co.uk
For jobs in the leisure industry worldwide.

Books

Introducing CBT: A Practical Guide, I. Foreman and
C. Pollard, London: Icon, 2011

Stop Worrying, A. Kerkhof, New York: McGraw-Hill/Open
University, 2010

Change Your Life with CBT, C. Sweet, Harlow: Pearson
Education, 2010

Cognitive Behavioural Therapy for Dummies, R. Willson
and R. Branch, Chichester: John Wiley & Sons Limited,
2006

An Introduction to CBT, D. Westbrook, H. Kennerley and
J. Kirk, London: Sage Publications, 2007

Entitled to Respect, S. Potts, Oxford: How to Books, 2010

Strong Imagination, D. Nettle, Oxford: Oxford University
Press, 2002

*Authentic Happiness, Using the New Positive Psychology
to Realise Your Potential for Lasting Fulfilment*, M.E.P.
Seligman, New York: Free Press, 2003

The Pleasures and Sorrows of Work, A. De Botton,
London: Hamish Hamilton, 2000

The Consolations of Philosophy, A. De Botton, London: Penguin, 2002

The Philosophy of Cognitive Behavioural Therapy (CBT): Stoic Philosophy as Rational and Cognitive Psychotherapy, D. Robertson, London: Karnac Books Ltd, 2010

Introducing Mindfulness: A Practical Guide, T. Watt, London: Icon, 2010

Positive Psychology, Y. Grenville-Cleave, London: Icon, 2012

Introducing Psychology of Success, A & D. Price, London: Icon, 2011

Introducing Sport Psychology, A. Leunes, London: Icon, 2011

Introducing Child Psychology, K. Cullen, London: Icon, 2011

Teach Yourself Managing Stress T. Looker and O. Gregson, London: Hodder Press, 1997

Work–Life Balance, G & R. Lamont, London: Sheldon Press, 2001

Overcoming Anger, when anger helps and when it hurts
W. Dryden, London: Sheldon Press, 1996

Overcoming Depression, W. Dryden and S. Opie, London:
Sheldon Press, 2003

Depression and How to Survive it, S. Milligan and A. Clare,
London: Random House, 1994

Overcoming Anxiety, W. Dryden, London: Sheldon Press,
2009

*How to be Your Own Best Friend, Overcoming Common
Problems*, P. Hauck, London: Sheldon Press, 1988

A Guide to Personal Happiness, A. Ellis and A. Becker,
Hollywood: United States, 1982

The 'Luck Factor' the Scientific Study of the Lucky Mind,
R. Wiseman, London: Arrow, 2004

Overcoming Health Anxiety, D. Veale and R. Wilson,
London: Robinson, 2009

The Mindful way Through Depression, M. Williams,
Z. Segal and J. Kabat-Zinn, London: Piatkus, 2007

Mindfulness for Beginners, J. Kabat-Zinn, Kindle Edition: Amazon EU, 2012

Mindfulness-Based Cognitive Therapy for Depression: A New Approach to Preventing Relapse, Z. Segal, J.M. Williams and J.D. Teasdale, Guilford Press, 2002

Index

Notes

You can use the following pages to make your own notes on any of the exercises in the book.

Notes

Notes

Notes

Notes

Notes

Notes

Notes

Notes

Notes

Other titles in
the Practical Guides series

A Practical Guide to Assertiveness

ISBN: 9781785783319
eISBN: 9781848315228

A Practical Guide to Child Psychology

ISBN: 9781785783227
eISBN: 9781848313293

A Practical Guide to Emotional Intelligence

ISBN: 9781785783234
eISBN: 9781848314382

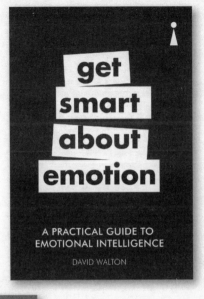

A Practical Guide to Ethics for Everyday Life

ISBN: 9781785783302
eISBN: 9781848313712

A Practical Guide to Happiness

ISBN: 9781785783241
eISBN: 9781848313637

A Practical Guide to Leadership

ISBN: 9781785783296
eISBN: 9781848315280

A Practical Guide to NLP for Work

ISBN: 9781785783265
eISBN: 9781848313811

A Practical Guide to Philosophy for Everyday Life

ISBN: 9781785783258
eISBN: 9781848313576

A Practical Guide to Productivity

ISBN: 9781785783326
eISBN: 9781848316973

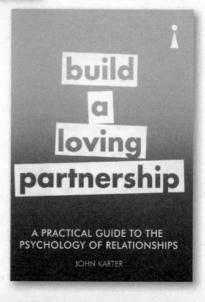

A Practical Guide to the Psychology of Relationships

ISBN: 9781785783289
eISBN: 9781848313606

**A Practical Guide to
Sport Psychology**

ISBN: 9781785783272
eISBN: 9781848313279

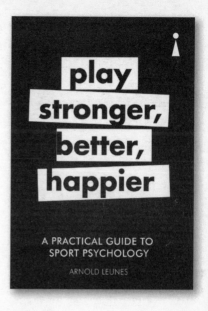

play
stronger,
better,
happier

A PRACTICAL GUIDE TO
SPORT PSYCHOLOGY

ARNOLD LEUNES